365 WAYS TO LOVE YOUR CHILD

365 WAYS TO L♥VE YOUR CHILD

Special Ways to Say I Love You:
- ♥ On Happy Days
- ♥ On Sad Days
- ♥ On Holidays
- ♥ EVERY DAY!

CARYL WALLER KRUEGER

ABINGDON PRESS / Nashville

365 WAYS TO LOVE YOUR CHILD

Copyright © 1994 by Caryl Waller Krueger

This book is printed on acid-free, recycled paper.

Library of Congress Cataloging-in-Publication Data

Krueger, Caryl Waller, 1929–
    365 ways to love your child / Caryl Waller Krueger.
      p.   cm.
    Includes index.
    ISBN 0-687-41891-7 (alk. paper)
    1. Parent and child—Miscellanea.   I. Title.
HQ755.85.K78   1994
306.874—dc20   93-44083

The author has made every effort to make the information and suggestions in this book practical and workable, but neither she nor the publisher assumes any responsibility for successes, failures, or other results of putting these ideas into practice.

Some of the ideas in this book are adapted from the author's previous books published by Abingdon Press, and from her *Six Weeks to Better Parenting* (Pelican Publishing Company, 1985).

Other books by Caryl Waller Krueger include:
1001 Things to Do with Your Kids (Abingdon Press)
Working Parent—Happy Child (Abingdon Press)
The Ten Commandments for Grandparents (Abingdon Press)
101 Ideas for the Best-ever Christmas (Dimensions for Living)
Single with Children (Abingdon Press)

94 95 96 97 98 99 00 01 02 03 04—10 9 8 7 6 5 4 3 2 1

MANUFACTURED IN THE UNITED STATES OF AMERICA

To

my nieces,

Nancy, Robin, Piper, Donna, Debbie, Connie & Merrie,

who, along with their husbands,

are guiding their children with love

CONTENTS

ACKNOWLEDGMENTS

*M*any thanks to these parents who shared their loving ideas with me: Robert Baer, Linda Bargmann, Gloria and Bob Brewster, Sally Buttner, Janet Faure, Evy Froehlich, Marty Fraser, Gordon Greeley, Berniece Hahn, Shirley Hoadley, Piper and Bruce Hunter, Craig Hunter, Robin Hunter, Connie King, Carrie Krueger, Bryan Landberg, Joyce Langton, Jean Mosteller, Carleen Pertschuk, Gwen McCauley, David Morris, Marie Newcom, Elieth Robertshaw, Ellen Sue Sarture, Susan and John Shaw, Joan Smutny, Deborah Simmons, Margaret Ellen Voss, Gloria Walters, and Colin Young, and write your own name here: _____ because you do loving things with your child each day.

INTRODUCTION
MAKING THE WORLD GO 'ROUND...

*L*ove not only makes the world go 'round—as it says in the song—but love also holds the world together.

It's the glue of families, communities, and nations. If love was a prime motive in every life, there wouldn't be petty disagreements or catastrophic wars.

All-encompassing, tender love starts the first time you hold your child in your arms. Yet expressions of love shouldn't end with babyhood; as children grow, we just need to work harder to find varied ways of showing our love.

Certainly spending time together and enjoying activities together are ways of demonstrating love within the family. Many such ideas were covered in my book *1001 Things to Do with Your Kids*. Now this new book describes very specific ways to simply love your child. If you make an effort to use these ideas for sharing love each day, this book will last you a year or more. You will find the results satisfying to both you and your child.

There is no greater gift than to love and to be loved.

365 WAYS!

♥

Note: The varied use of she *and* he *in referring to youngsters has no relevance to the idea. The words* he *and* she *should be thought of as interchangeable. If an idea doesn't seem pertinent to your child's age, consider modifying it. In parenting, creativity is the name of the game!*

♥ 1 THE SPECIAL PLATE

When a child has done something special, or feels hurt, or seems to need love for any reason, serve her dinner on "The Special Plate." Although you can buy plates that say "You are special," you can also have a good time (and save money) by letting each child pick out her own plate at a secondhand store or garage sale. One youngster found a plate with a real gold edge for just fifty cents, and another found one with an authentic Native American design. When their meal is served on these plates, they feel truly special.

♥ 2 ONCE A DAY

*A*s you say goodnight to your youngster, think back over the day's events. Whether it was a day of disaster or harmony, you can still end the day on a loving note. Get up from the sofa, take time to walk to a child's room, give a hug and a kiss and tell that child how much you treasure him. Never let the day end without this expression of love. (This works well on spouses, too!)

♥ 3 LOVE THIS HOUSE

*Y*our house may not be big or fancy, but love it just the same. Use every corner of it: picnic in the living room, roast marshmallows in the fireplace, put on swim suits and use paper cups for a water fight in the tub/shower, sleep overnight in sleeping bags under the dining room table, have a pillow fight in the bedroom, see who can put the best picture or message on the refrigerator door, start a crafts corner in the garage. Your home is a big investment, so enjoy it with the folks who live inside.

♥ 4 GOOD-MORNING PANCAKES

*S*tart the day with love! Make simple pancakes, but just before flipping them (when the batter is almost set on top) use a knife to draw a heart on the pancake. It only takes a few seconds, but it sends a good message.

♥ 5 PARAMETERS

*W*ith your youngster, look up this word in the dictionary. Tell her that because you love her, you are setting some parameters to her activities. Let her help write these "Loving Limits." They might include rules on telephone use, snacks, homework, weekday social events, curfew, driving, dating, drinking, drugs, smoking, ear-piercing, church attendance, room care, chores—whatever is pertinent to her age.

♥ 6 WHISPERS

*N*ot all family conversations have to be heard by everyone. Whisper a love message in a child's ear as he leaves for school, goes out to play, does his homework, goes to bed. Follow your whispered message with a soft kiss.

♥ 7 HAND-ME-DOWN JEWELRY

*B*oth mom and dad should check their jewelry boxes for something that is still good, but that they no longer wear. Then, when there is an occasion (learning to ride a bike, being in a play, first date, great grades, getting a driver's license, graduation) or just a time when you want a child to know you love and appreciate him, present one of these heirlooms that is appropriate to his age.

♥ 8   LOVABLE ART WORK

*B*uy some inexpensive frames or make them of cardboard. When a child brings home from school a good paper or drawing, frame it and hang it up. Change the hangings regularly. Show you appreciate good effort at school.

♥ 9   YOU LOVE MY IDEA?

*S*ometimes kids come up with rather bizarre ideas. It could be easy to make fun of the idea, or simply rule it out as impossible. It takes parental loving respect to carefully consider a request that seems out-landish. But if it isn't totally inappropriate, dangerous, or illegal, try to say "yes"! You don't have a corner on all good ideas.

♥ 10   WATCHDOGS

*E*ncourage kids to take an interest in the activities of their sib-lings—to become sensitive watchdogs. When you suggest to them a way to help or show affection, give lots of praise when they follow through. As an example, you might say: "Jeremy has a big test tomorrow. Why don't you see if he'd like you to feed the dog and set the table for him. I'm sure there will be a time when you might need some extra help." Or, a child might see that the Sunday paper is spread over the floor and just pick it up without being asked. That's a real watchdog! To do the loving, helpful thing should be natural; it doesn't need a chart or a reminder or a reward.

♥ 11 COOKIE MAKER

*W*hen a friend isn't feeling well, or when there are newcomers or senior citizens in the neighborhood, work as a parent/youth team to make cookies. Help a young child deliver them; a teen can do it on his own. It's important that your child sees your care for others, so that he in turn can be caring. When there's a new student at school, take the cookies and some juice and go with your child for a short visit to that family. Parents can chat while the kids serve the refreshments; this breaks the ice in conversation. Giving love and being loved often go hand in hand.

♥ 12 RESOLUTIONS

*O*n New Year's Day—or some other day if you choose—gather the family to discuss resolutions and goals for the year ahead. Helping youngsters plan ahead is a sign of your care for them and the family. Decide first on resolutions for the entire family: For example, to share some good news (not just problems) each day, to have a day of rest each week, to do something outdoors each weekend, to communicate with relatives regularly, to eat dinner together each night, to read every day. Then, each family member decides on individual goals, such as to learn a new sport, to make a new friend, to improve a grade, to contribute a new idea at the office, to get rid of a bad habit. Write down all the resolutions. On the first of each month, bring them out and see how everyone is doing.

17

♥ 13 BORROW A BABY

*C*aring for a baby can be fun and educational, and "borrowing" one for a few hours lets another parent have some free time. (Of course, you'll need to see that family members understand the needs of the baby.) It's a wonderful way to show the other busy parent that you care, and it's an opportunity for you and your child to show love. Of course, you'll be on the scene, but let your own child help as much as she's able. Remind your child that when she was little, you held and hugged her the same way.

♥ 14 RISE AND SHINE

*A*waken your child—or better yet, let an alarm clock do the awakening—early enough each morning so that you don't have to be reminding and rushing him through this important time. Make your first words to your child *calm and cheerful* ones, to start his day off right.

♥ 15 ROOTS AND WINGS

*T*here are two things we give a child. The first is roots: a deep understanding of your confidence in his abilities and your unconditional love. The other is wings: the right to use those abilities on his own because you want him to gain his independence.

18

♥ 16 BECAUSE

*W*hile we may not always *like* what our child is doing, we always love her and want her to know it. Parents and kids should use "I love you" every day so that the words are part of family vocabulary. Then add the word *because* and complete the sentence: " . . . because you're so funny"; " . . . because you're you"; " . . . because you said you were sorry"; " . . . because you're special."

♥ 17 THE CASTLE

*T*oddler or teen, a youngster's room is an important place—a place he should love. (That's why you don't send kids to their rooms as punishment.) Visit a child's room daily, knocking first if the door is closed. Their "turf" is a good environment for both tender and serious conversations. It's an ideal place to remind a youngster of your love.

♥ 18 LOVE GRANDMA; HELP GRANDMA

*G*randparents do many loving things for their grandchildren, so let the kids do loving things in return. At the home of one grandpa, there are two colors of small stones in the front yard. One little grandson likes to return wayward stones to their proper place. A teenager is a "repair person" and changes faucet washers, light bulbs, and does other minor repairs from a grandma's list. At another home, a grandson programs the VCR each week for later viewing.

♥ 19 FAX ME YOUR LOVE

A mom has a FAX machine and so does her own father, the grandpa. Once when one of his granddaughters was in an essay contest, she told him she was sure she would win. Although she worked very hard, she came in second and was quite depressed. The grandpa sent a FAX picture he'd drawn, showing himself and his granddaughter hugging, and it was labeled: "You're always the winner with me." It was just the love message she needed to snap out of the blues.

♥ 20 MAKE UP A LOVE SONG

*U*sing a familiar tune, make up a simple song about how much you love your child. Here's one set to the tune of "You Are My Sunshine."

> You are my Claire Bear, my little Claire Bear
> You make me happy the whole day through
> You'll never know, Claire, how much I love you
> Please remember I love all you do.

♥ 21 HAVE YOU HUGGED A TREE LATELY?

*W*hen in the park or walking down the sidewalk together, count how many trees you can hug *together*. (Your hands and your child's hands must meet around the tree trunk.) Each time your hands meet, say, "I like this tree, but I love you so much more."

♥ 22 FEARS ARE FOES

*I*f your child is afraid of someone or something, take the time to help him overcome it; don't ridicule a child's fears. In a crowd, hold your child's hand securely so he won't fear being separated or lost.

♥ 23 MARTIN LUTHER KING DAY

*M*any folks miss the point of this newest national holiday. Set aside life-styles and politics and help your youngsters focus on the message: equality and love for *all humankind*. Point up the importance of these two issues to your children. Read a summary of black history from the encyclopedia or other reference book. Discuss how the newspaper covers this holiday. Consider how your family or your church can help repair the separation between the races.

♥ 24 AND THEN THERE ARE ABE AND GEORGE

*T*oo often kids only know that it's a day off from school when the presidents' birthdays are celebrated. Reinforce school training by talking about patriotism and love of country. Your love for your country and your love for your child can result in good conversation about democracy.

♥ 25 THE LOVE PLANT

*W*hen a new family moved in, a caring next-door neighbor noticed the loneliness of the only child, a little boy. It was then she invented the "Love Plant." She brought over a pot with good soil in it, along with a morning glory seed. Although she didn't tell him what the seed was, she told him that he should plant and care for the seed. She said it was a "Love Plant" and that it would grow and be beautiful and people would certainly notice it. She added that in the same way, the boy was going to grow in his new neighborhood and he would be handsome and noticed by others. The boy didn't think that would happen, but by the time the plant had climbed its string and produced beautiful blue flowers, he realized that he had made many friends, and was not lonely any more. He grew morning glory seeds every year as a remembrance of the neighbor's caring.

♥ **26** CHANGE THE ENVIRONMENT

*S*ometimes conflict develops when siblings get bored. You can return youngsters to more caring relationships with each other by changing the environment. This could involve merely taking the same game or toys to another room, turning off the TV and turning on music, or introducing some new element to their play. When a parent does not respond to kids' arguments with shouts but rather speaks kindly, softly, and calmly, the situation can change easily. Use the phrase "I love you both too much to let you do this to each other."

♥ **27** REALLY CHANGE THE ENVIRONMENT

*L*ove within the family needs to spread to the world. Yes, *you* can love the environment. Get one of the many good books for kids on how to change the environment and save the world. Show your love for the world by doing your part in recycling, appreciating the outdoors without trashing it, planting trees, using less energy, and so forth. Using the book as a guide, work together as a family to make a specific list of what you plan to do.

♥ 28 ALL-ALONE BOX

*W*ith a child's help, select some of her toys that are best played with when alone. Put them in a basket or a carton that the child can color or decorate with hearts and flowers. Then add the toys and put the collection on a top shelf or other out-of-the-way place. When a child feels lonely or must play alone, bring out the "All-alone Box." Its novelty will hold her interest and alleviate her boredom.

♥ 29 GIVING THANKS

*D*iscuss with your child the importance of gratitude. (A grateful and appreciative child will be a social winner!) Of course, verbal thanks *within* the family is a good place to start. And this should be extended to relatives and friends, teachers and scout leaders, and so forth. A little practice will help a child to be comfortable when expressing thanks for a dinner, a movie, or a gift. Be specific in going over the polite words with a young child. Thank-you notes are another requirement. Those too young to write them can draw a picture. Children should write a sentence for each year of their age, with ten being the maximum required. Be sure you set the example of gratitude yourself.

♥ 30 ADOPT A PET

*J*ust waiting for love are the many pets at Humane Societies and animal shelters. When you go to adopt a pet, choose one that has a history of being good with children, rather than a stray with no history. If it's a dog, ask to take it out onto a grassy area to romp with the children. See how it responds to its name, or the throwing of a ball. While a pet often means more work for a parent, it is also a sign that the parent loves a child enough to take on this extra work. Before making the adoption official, decide what care the pet will need and just how those tasks are to be accomplished each day by the youngsters.

♥ 31 "LOVE" DOESN'T MEAN "LET"

*D*on't confuse love with permissiveness. Sometimes letting a child do something you don't really approve of erodes your relationship and harms the child. Sometimes telling a child *no* is the most loving thing you can do for him. True love is not inhibiting; it loosens a child to do his best. When you loosen a child, you will not lose him; he will be all the more bound to you in love.

♥ 32 SATURDAY WRESTLING

*W*hile it's best to have kids sleep in their own beds, it can be fun to occasionally wrestle and have pillow fights in your bed. Saturday is a good time to let everyone pile in the parents' bed. Start with sleepy hugs, then tickling and wrestling for those who like it, and finally throwing those pillows around.

♥ 33 OH, REALLY?

*W*hen a tattletale comes to you with bad news, first give him a hug. That will let him know you care about him—although you may not approve of his complaint. With the hug, say "Oh, really? Now why do you think Mikey did that?" This will help the tattletale figure out how the problem got started, and perhaps how to solve it.

♥ 34 FINE TUNING

*T*he taller the child, the less we listen—so goes the research. Also, what we hear may not be the real message a child is sending. A sharing/listening/responding relationship is indispensable to a child's confidence about her own identity and a conviction about her basic rights as a member of the family and the community. While peer listening often includes judging, adult/child listening includes perceptiveness and love. Just the willingness of an adult to listen bolsters a child's sense of security and conscious worth.

♥ 35 SHARING AND CARING

*M*ake opportunities to share. Let a child cut one cupcake in half, knowing that you (or someone else) will get to choose your half first. Show how to use a timer so that everyone gets to use a favorite toy. Visually or by words, show that loving one another is very important. Make a little chart and use different colored stars for achievements: red for doing chores, green for reading a book, silver for nutritious eating, and a much larger gold star for specific times of sharing and caring.

♥ 36 THE LOVE BUNNY

*L*ittle children usually have many, many stuffed toys. When a child gets tired of one, give it a new look. This works with a bunny or another animal that has light-colored fur. Using a wide red marking pen, draw a big heart on the bunny's chest. Write in it "I love (the child's name)." Then refer to it as the love bunny, or the love bear.

♥ 37 GOOD NEWS

*W*hen your youngster has done something especially good or kind, don't keep the good news to yourself. Telephone it to a spouse at work (who may be able to call the child and congratulate him) or phone or write a relative, who may in turn phone or write the youngster.

♥ 38 LOVE POEM

*H*olding your left hand palm up, take your thumb and touch it to each of your four fingers (on the same hand) as you teach this poem to your child. Then show the child how to use his fingers the same way. The word *mama,* of course, can be changed.

Mama loves me naughty or nice. (Touch thumb to little finger.)
Mama sometimes kisses me twice. (Touch thumb to index finger.)
Mama hugs me when work is done. (Touch thumb to middle finger.)
Mama cuddles me just for fun. (Touch thumb to ring finger.)

♥ 39 "I'D LOVE TO!"

*P*opularize this phrase as a family saying. Start out by encouraging it during children's play together. Tell them to let you know when they've said it. Being agreeable can be a sign of caring. Use it yourself

when asked to do something. Another good phrase is "No problem."
When asked to do something, a "no problem" response is reassuring.

♥ **40** OUT ON THE TOWN

*L*ittle children often feel clingy and sad when parents are
going out for the evening without them. Let your son be dad's valet or a
daughter your makeup assistant. A little girl likes to prance around in
high heels or a son likes to practice tying a tie. Use this time to talk to
your child about where you're going, what you'll do, and when you'll be
home.

♥ **41** YOUR BABY'S STORY

*T*ell your child the story of how she came to be part of the family. (Never tell a child she was a "surprise"—every child needs to be
wanted and loved.) If you kept a baby book, look through it together. Tell
how you chose her name. One mother who adopted a baby from a faraway country wrote a true-story book called *The Empty Cradle,* which
told of her search for a baby, the trip to the foreign country to adopt her,
the long return trip, and finally the welcome when they returned home—
when the cradle was no longer empty.

♥ 42 VALENTINE'S DAY

*H*ere's a holiday built on love—so really celebrate it! Let kids make and decorate a Valentine box for the center of the eating table. Encourage the making of handmade cards. Put these cards and some small wrapped gifts inside the box. Write a love letter to each child, telling him all the ways he's special to you. At supper on Valentine's Day, open the box and distribute the contents one at a time. Serve a red-and-white meal: red gelatin, white chicken, red beets or tomatoes, white potatoes, red and white cake with pink milk. Look up Saint Valentine in the encyclopedia and discuss how the family can be more caring.

♥ 43 VALENTINE OR ANYTIME

*S*ome people buy a billboard to tell someone they love them. Others put the message on a banner from an airplane. Let your youngster put the message on your sidewalk. Being a sidewalk Rembrandt works equally well on a patio, safe driveway, or even some basement floors. You'll need a small bucket, some *watercolor* paints, and inexpensive paint brushes, large and small. First, put a little paint on the surface and be sure it comes off with water. Then, patiently paint with a plan. (You can also paint with water alone, and while this is fun, the message disappears as the water dries up.) Paint people, houses, trees, airplanes. Once you have the knack, you can write messages, make sidewalk Valentines, do addition problems, make cartoons. Surprise a working parent with a loving welcome-home message on the front sidewalk!

♥ 44 HELP FROM ABOVE

*S*how your youngster how much you care by telling him that you pray for him each day. Help him to put his needs into words of prayer.

♥ 45 WRITE INSTEAD OF TALK

*S*eeing something has a more lasting effect than just hearing it. That's why you'll want to occasionally write a love note to your child. A compliment or words of reassurance of your love no-matter-what can be a great comfort. And when it is in writing, it can be read over and over again.

♥ 46 DEDICATE A BOOK

*W*hen you give a child a book, write a message of love on the blank page up near the front. Write it near the top of the page. Encourage the recipient to feel free to dedicate the book to another reader when he's finished reading it. Some books will have quite a history of inscriptions.

♥ 47 BAN THE BLAME

*Y*ou don't need to pin a child to the wall with blame. So often mornings begin with shouts like "Because you overslept, you're going to be late!" This hardly starts a youngster's morning with a feeling of family affection. Instead, use facts to replace words of blame. Better to say: "It's 7:15 and your school bus will be here in just thirty minutes."

♥ 48 "I'M HOME!"

*W*henever your child comes home (from school, or from play, or from a date), stop what you're doing and greet her with a hug, showing her that you're delighted to see her. Don't just call "hello" from another room or neglect to acknowledge her return.

♥ 49 PRECIOUS POSSESSIONS

*W*hen children are going to have a new experience (an overnight with a friend, a camp-out, a train trip), let them take something familiar with them. The take-along might be a stuffed animal or doll, a favorite shirt, a photo of the family, a well-loved book, or something small that fits in a pocket. Children are often fearful, and your understanding love means a lot.

♥ 50 MAIL CALL

*L*et your preschooler help you sort the daily mail. Some of the catalogs you don't want can be his own mail. Tell him to find pictures that show people having fun, parents loving their children, or clothes he'd like to wear some day. He might like to color on the pages, too, adding to the pictures.

♥ 51 TWO LITTLE WORDS

*S*ay thank you often so a child knows you don't take her actions for granted. Even thank her for doing her chores. A thank-you with a smile or an arm around her shoulders can mean a lot.

♥ 52 TAKE FIVE!

*S*ometimes the entire family needs a breather. Everyone is frantically doing chores or homework, and things are tense. Teach family members to notice this strained behavior and shout "Take five!"—the cue for everyone to relax. The shouter can suggest a cold drink, a run around the house, simple floor exercise, followed by an all-family hug before going back to work.

♥ 53 A VOICE FOR CHOICE

*T*here are some tasks that just must be done by kids. You'll be most effective at getting their cooperation if you give them two specific choices such as: "Do you want to see a half-hour of TV first, or empty the dishwasher first?" "Do you want to clean up your room now or after you call Marcy?" The phrase "Do you want" is very important, for it shows youngsters that you love them enough to trust their decisions.

♥ 54 G & G CHEER UP

*W*hen a child is feeling low, let him make a phone call to a grandparent. Or the call can be made to a PGP (a proxy grandparent), a caring neighbor or friend. A phone call often makes a child feel loved and good about herself.

♥ 55 LOST AND FOUND

*W*hen a child is distressed over losing something, stop and help him look for it. Remember, if it is important to your child, it should be important to you. And, if you happen to find it first, lead him to the place where he'll discover it himself.

♥ 56 CHEWY TREATS

A wrapped stick of sugar-free gum can be a happy little message of love. Use it as a placemark in a book a youngster is reading, or in the back of a toy truck, or in the hand of a favorite doll.

♥ 57 LOVE THAT EDUCATES

*I*n the grade school years, subjects such as premarital sex, AIDS, venereal disease, abortion, and abstinence *must* be discussed between parents and children. Don't count on the school to cover these topics relative to your own family's values. Because your child is so dear to you, you want him to have correct up-to-date information so he can live a long, healthy, and happy life. Keep the lines of communication open by being frank and by calmly answering all questions.

♥ 58 POINTED PRAISE

*O*f course we all like compliments when we've accomplished something or made an effort. Too often, though, such appreciation is in general terms. Praise has a more lasting effect when it is specific. "Thank you for emptying the dishwasher, and it was great that you found the place I keep the pie pans." "It was super that you got a B-plus, but I'm especially pleased with all you learned about President Andrew Jackson."

♥ 59 WHEREVER YOU GO

*T*ake a blanket outside so you can lie down and look at the stars. With your youngsters, talk about astronauts walking on the moon and voyages into space. Discuss how the parents of the astronauts feel when their children actually leave this planet. Tell your kids that wherever they go, you will always love them.

♥ 60 A TRUE LOVE STORY

♥ *LOVE IN THE WILDERNESS* ♥

Everything about Daniel's home was up-to-date. As an only child, he had most everything he wanted, yet he wasn't spoiled. But he was puzzled about what to do for his thirteenth summer. He wanted this summer to be unique, different from tennis lessons or horseback riding at camp.

In May, before school let out, his mother suggested a summer in the wilderness—a test of survival. But, and this is what stunned him, he would be going with his mother! It wouldn't be a group event, just the two of them against the elements. His father apologized for being too busy at his job, but wholeheartedly supported his wife, saying: "She's an amazing woman . . . if I had to be a castaway on an island, she's the one I'd want along!"

So, the day after school ended, they loaded the car, his father waved them off and his best friend Mark stood in the driveway shouting, "Let me know when you've learned to survive out there—then I'll come and visit!"

As the roads got narrower and dustier, Daniel wondered if this was such a hot idea. Yet, as he asked question after question, his mother remained calm, going over the plans with him. She said this was going to be a summer they'd both remember . . . and Daniel prayed the memories would be good! A rancher had given them permission to make their camp on some unused land by a stream. And the first night, with food from home and a full moon, it seemed idyllic.

But then came the survival test. The next morning they were up early and she gave him a brief lesson on fishing, saying, "No fish, no breakfast!" And by late afternoon she announced, "No rabbit, no dinner!" He always knew his mother loved hiking and sailing, but he had never seen this determined pioneering side of her. But she was no novice with pole or gun and soon he was preparing meals with the skills she taught by patient demonstration.

After two weeks, they were confident enough to tell Mark that they were surviving and he should come. By now, the campsite was like home—comfortable, clean, and well-supplied with games and books. Mark marveled at this private wilderness he was sharing with his friend. Days were spent hiking to spectacular viewpoints and splashing in the stream. Evenings included games and conversation (mostly about girls and dating since the threesome found it easy to talk about this all-important topic in the dark). Each night, Dan fell asleep under a canopy of stars and thought about his life ahead. He wanted it to always be an adventure like this.

So, the summer became a three-month lesson in botany, astronomy, getting-along, hunting, skinning rabbits, deboning fish, devising pranks, cooking, and planning—most of which Dan showed off to his father on the two weekends when he could join them. He sadly counted down the days until school would start again. He realized how special it was, to be able to share these memories with two best friends—Mark and Mom—and that his mother loved him so much that she give him this most memorable summer.

♥ 61 A FEW OF THOSE FAVORITE THINGS

*A*ll of us have favorites. We like chocolate cake or the color blue or supper by the fire. Talk about favorite things at supper and let everyone tell theirs. Write them down and post them on the bulletin board. Then, when you—or another family member—want to do something loving and thoughtful, you'll have some good ideas to choose from.

♥ 62 SHIFT THE RESPONSIBILITY

*A*s youngsters grow, we should be doing less and less for them so that they will be ready to totally take care of themselves. However, our love for them sometimes gets in the way and we take on activities they should do on their own. If a child has left his school books at the public library say: "I think it would be a good idea for you to call the library right now. I'm sure they have your books and you can cycle over to get them." (Here you've planted the thought that it's a good idea.) Or when a youngster wants to practice golf in the backyard, say, "You have my permission to dig a hole in the lawn, put a can in it, and practice putting." (Here you've used that wonderful word *permission*.) Or when a youngster wants to buy a bike to replace the one he lost, you can say "You can save money by checking the newspaper for a good second-hand bike." (*Save money* are magic words to a youngster with limited funds.) Let your youngsters become self-governing by doing more and more on their own.

♥ 63 HEART-TO-HEART CAKE

*I*t doesn't have to be a birthday to have a cake. Jazz up a cake mix and then decorate a cake for a member of the family who needs a little TLC. Keep it a surprise. After supper, put a few candles on the cake and let the recipient serve it.

♥ 64 PICTURE YOUR CHILD

*T*hink about your child in your "mind's eye." When you visualize a child as caring and competent and successful, you treat her that way and she responds in kind. Don't label a child as lazy, naughty, or mean—don't label her in words or in your thoughts. "What you see is what you get" may be a pop phrase, but it's also a true one concerning our expectations for our children.

♥ 65 "MORNING SEVENS"

*A*n independent child is almost always a happy child. Show your youngster that you care about his becoming self-governing by giving him a list of the seven things he should do first thing each morning: go to the bathroom, wash, dress, make bed, tidy room, do one chore, brush teeth after breakfast.

♥ 66 BULLIES

*N*o one likes a bully. We tell our children not to be bullies or let their friends bully them. Yet, there are times when we are bullying parents. It's better to rule by love than by fear. Intimidating statements have these phrases in them: "You must . . . ," "Don't you ever . . . ," "I'm telling . . . ," "If you don't . . . ," "Don't ask . . . ," "Shut up and do it," "I don't want to hear . . . ."

39

♥ 67 USING SICK TIME

*D*on't let illness be an excuse for days of mindless television viewing. Try to interest a youngster in activities that tie in with her normal routine. This could be getting dressed for supper, doing some homework, making a phone call to a friend, playing with the dog in her room, helping a parent with a project that can be done on the bedspread. Give her extra love as you ease her back into the normal routine of family life.

♥ 68 LIGHT UP THOSE BURGERS

A meal seems special when there are candles. But they don't have to be on a cake. When serving hamburgers (or other suitable foods such as baked potatoes), put a candle in the center of each one. This touch will make eaters of all ages feel special, and somehow, the food will taste even better.

♥ 69 ADOPT A CHILD BY MAIL

*O*ur supply of love is unlimited, so show your older child how to share it by adopting a child by mail. There are many agencies that provide care for children overseas as well as some nearer home. The monthly contribution is not great and all the family can share in paying for it.

Ask for a child similar in age to your own. Most important is the exchange of letters. In return for your letters, you'll receive regular letters that will give you clues about your adopted child's way of life, education, interests, and needs. In compliance with agency guidelines, you may be able to provide books or other small gifts for the child's birthday or for a holiday. With your child, learn about the country where your adopted child lives. Put the child's picture on your bulletin board. Some of these relationships continue for many years, and your family will have the joy of making a real contribution to another's life.

♥ 70 MEMORIAL-DAY MEMORIES

*T*his holiday, often called Decoration Day, honors those who have died defending the United States. Some families go to cemeteries to place flowers on family graves. Show your love for those relatives and friends who have passed on by turning the focus away from death toward a commemoration of those who have been an important part of the family and community. You may want to attend a ceremony at a military cemetery—these can be very moving. Show your children the importance of living our lives in such a way as to make a difference to society so that we will be remembered by the good we accomplished.

♥ 71 THE FAMILY CROWN

*W*ork together with a youngster to make a crown out of cardboard and aluminum foil. Make it "uni-size," with a clip to adjust it at the back. Then explain the rules for the family crown. When someone has done something special, or when someone needs a little tender care, he gets to wear the crown. Teach children to crown each other. It's a nice way to share your caring.

♥ 72 THE GOLDEN RULE

*I*n many religions and philosophies, some form of the golden rule is a standard for civilized living. Teach this rule to your youngster and encourage adherence to it. It is a strong declaration of love for one another: "Do unto others as you would have them do unto you." You may want to paraphrase it: "Love others as you would be loved."

♥ 73 OOPS

*D*on't spend much of your talking time being critical. Too much censure gets in the way of love. Still, some things must be corrected. Using a few large pieces of cardboard, write OOPS on each one. Then, when you see something that you might nag about, put a sign there—by the food left out, the TV left on, the messy room, the towel on the bathroom door. Make a home for your OOPS signs so that they can be returned when the problem is corrected (and so you can use them again!). Kids will appreciate your kind, nonverbal correction. And you might find an OOPS sign next to your own mess some day!

♥ 74 SOMETHING YOU CAN'T GIVE

*T*here's a lot of talk about *giving* self-worth and self-esteem to a youngster. But you can't just bestow esteem; it must come from within. It is the result of a youngster's positive daily experiences. So what you *can* give is opportunities to gain self-worth. These opportunities include making decisions (and possibly suffering the consequences), taking responsibility, finishing tasks, completing homework, volunteering help, caring for others. It's up to you to then notice these achievements and comment favorably on them.

♥ 75 GRANDPARENTS' SHOPPING SERVICE

*S*ometimes young children like to tangibly show that they love their parents by giving a gift, but often they don't have the opportunity to go shopping. Grandparents can help by providing an occasion to take the child to the store or mall. Look for a good but useful bargain (the grandparents may have to help subsidize the purchase). Help with the wrapping and give ideas for making a card that expresses the child's feelings.

43

♥ 76 A LOVE KIT

*W*hen a friend is in the hospital or ill at home, let your child help put together a "Love Kit." A piece of fresh fruit, a bottle of cologne, a paperback book, the TV listings from the newspaper, note cards with stamps on the envelopes, nail polish, a small mirror, a small game or crossword puzzle are some enclosures an adult would appreciate. For a child, consider a granola bar (depending on the illness), cartoons or a comic book, a small toy or truck that can be played with in bed, a magazine, a small puzzle, a music or story cassette. Suggest that your child make a loving get-well greeting card for the kit.

♥ 77 CARE ENOUGH

*L*ove protects! Show your children how much you care for them by keeping them very safe. Talk about these situations: when there is a fire in the house, when someone knocks on the door, when they're approached by a stranger, when they're home alone and the phone rings, when they see matches, poisons, guns, and so forth. Tell them that you want them to know about these things, not to make them afraid, but because you truly care for them and want them to always be safe.

♥ 78 FLOWER POWER

*T*oo often we only bring flowers into our house when company is coming. But the family should be equally important. If you don't have a small vase for just one flower, make one out of a tall, narrow olive jar. Tie a ribbon around the neck of the jar and hang on the ribbon a loving message. Pick just one flower for the vase and put it in a child's room. When the flower wilts, pick another and put the vase in a different room with a different love message.

♥ 79 CLOSE TO YOU

*F*ind occasions to be alone and sit close to your child. This could be on a loveseat, a porch swing, a hammock, or two of you in one chair. This closeness can bring about good conversation and a sharing of innermost thoughts and feelings.

♥ 80 LOVE PILLOW

*W*hen a youngster is learning to sew (and that means both boys and girls), show him how to make a special pillow to give to a sibling or grandparent, or to have in his own room. Using a pillow that has seen better days, make a covering for it out of an interesting new fabric or a

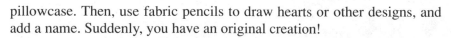

pillowcase. Then, use fabric pencils to draw hearts or other designs, and add a name. Suddenly, you have an original creation!

♥ 81 "YOU KNOW BEST"

*T*hose are wonderful words and show our trust in a growing child's good judgment. Show your faith by using "You know best" whenever there is a choice a youngster should make. For example, "I thought you'd want me to test you on your spelling words, but you know best how much help you need." Or, "That is a good looking shirt, but you know best as to whether you want this costly one instead of two that are less expensive." Letting him make choices gives a child a good feeling of your confidence and love.

♥ 82 "YOU LOOK MARVELOUS!"

*O*ne comic made that saying famous, and your family can benefit by using the line at your house. Everyone needs an upbeat send-off in the morning. So create a line for family members to use when they first see each other. "You look outrageous!" "You look fantastic!" "You look deeeeelightful!" "You look huggable!" Use the same line regularly, so it catches on.

♥ 83 HONESTY HURTS

*A*t times it takes courage to tell the truth, especially when a lie might have covered the situation. Be quick to compliment a child who has been honest. Put your arms around her and tell her how much you appreciate her honesty. Even though you may have to punish, be sure you make the point that punishment is always lighter when the truth is told.

♥ 84 LOVE VIDEOS

*S*et aside one videotape for each child. On it record his special events for the year: making Valentines, bike riding, birthday party, helping cook supper, teaching the dog a trick, opening his favorite Christmas present, and so forth. Then on New Year's Day, let all the youngsters see the wonderful times they've had during the previous 365 days.

♥ 85 WINNING AND LOSING

*S*o the team lost. Show your child that you're proud of her—and you love her—whether her team is the champ or not. Celebrate the sport and good sportsmanship at the ice-cream parlor or back home. Talk first about the things the team did well: good plays, scores, and the effort an exercise involved. If it fits into the conversation, also talk about respect for team players, what makes a good team member, what skills are needed to improve the team. Talk about the currently popular "trash talk" that goes on between players at sports events. Show it to be unkind, degrading, and unnecessary. Help your child to take consolation in old sayings, like "It's more important *how* you played the game."

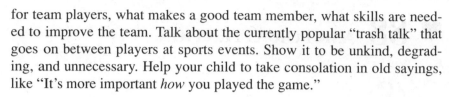

♥ 86 LOVABLE T-SHIRT

*B*efore a new baby comes, help older siblings make a special T-shirt, using an inexpensive plain white or pastel shirt and marking pens. Letter on the shirt: "I'm the BIG brother" or "I'm the BIG sister." (This is more fun than buying this kind of shirt ready-made.) Let the child decorate the shirt with a picture of a baby and X's and O's (hug and kiss signs).

♥ 87 DO IT *WITH*, NOT *TO*

*T*oo many parents are talking *to* their youngsters, doing corrective things *to* their children, and failing to have much fun *with* their kids. For one or two days, keep a tabulation as to how many activities are with your youngsters, as opposed to how many occasions you just give an order or briefly answer a question. Let's hope there are twice as many "withs" as there are "tos." For more ideas on good activities with children, read my book *1001 Things to Do with Your Kids* (Abingdon Press, 1988).

♥ **88** ASK FOR ATTENTION

*S*ometimes what seems like an unloving attitude is really a cry for attention. Teach children to *ask* for (not demand) attention when they need it, and in turn be sure to give 100 percent attention in response. This helps to recognize a child as an individual rather than as just part of the group called "the kids." In your daily unstructured time with a child, make sure that the greater part of it is spent doing things the child wants to do. Paying attention to a child as an individual pays big bonuses in child-to-child relationships as well as parent-to-child ones.

♥ **89** HUGGY PHOTOS

*F*ind a photo booth that provides multiple photos for very little money. Let everyone (or at least two of you) pile into the tiny booth for a close-together photo. Be giggly, be funny, be huggy. Put the photos up on the refrigerator door or bathroom mirror or give one to each youngster.

♥ **90** PROMISES

*W*hen taking a parent to the airport for a business trip, put the soon-to-be-away parent in the backseat with the kids. Parent and children can start sentences with the words "Do you promise . . . ." A child may think of things like: "Do you promise to call us tomorrow night . . . to send me a postcard . . . to think of me when you drink orange juice?" A parent may say: "Do *you* promise to think of *me* when you drink orange juice . . . blow me a kiss as you fall asleep . . . to help Grandma make cookies . . . to give the dog a hug?"

♥ 91 BIG BROTHER SAYS . . .

*S*tart teaching parenting skills early. Big brother, big sister, little brother, little sister can all have good ideas. When there is a problem, ask a sibling what he might do in a similar situation. The ideas may surprise you. One big brother told his little brother, "You're spending too much time on video games. Get your homework done and I'll take you outside and show you some pointers on the real game of baseball." Encouraging siblings to be mentors for one another increases peace and love in the family.

♥ 92 BEDTIME LOVE

*P*rovide these essentials for going to bed: a warm bath, a trip to the bathroom, a drink of water, a story, soft radio music or a music box, a bell at the bedside to call parents in case of emergency, a hug and a kiss. Then give reassurance: "All is well," "I love you," "See you in the morning," "It was a good day."

♥ 93 WHEN TWO TANGLE

*I*t may be hard to determine who is right and who is wrong. But perhaps *you* don't have to. Often you can turn the problem over to the youngsters and let them figure it out themselves without your arbitration. Instead of interrogation of each one, treat them as a team by saying "This is your problem so you settle it. If I get into it, I may be too strict." This shows you love them equally and want them to learn how to work together. To implement this, let them use a clock timer for taking turns in discussing the matter. Or, encourage the practice of their writing down their grievance (an activity that often shows how silly some arguments are). You encourage them to settle their own differences amicably when you move away from their action and let them talk things over themselves.

♥ 94 CLOCKS AND TICKETS FOR TOGETHERNESS

*W*hen you're busy and you have to put off a child's request to later in the day, note your good intentions right on the most noticeable clock in the house. Tape a little sign right next to the number seven or nine (or whenever you'll have time). Write on it "William's basketball time" or "Jessica's insect-hunting time." Be sure to follow through with your promise. Or give a child a "ticket for talk" (a three-by-five-inch index card with the topic printed on it). This shows your good intention to talk about the request as soon as possible, and that you're not just getting rid of her and hoping she'll forget. You may want to put on the card a time or day for the discussion.

♥ 95 TOASTING

*A*t mealtime, propose a sincere complimentary toast to a child. Do it when a child has had a success, or when a child needs to know you care. Tell about her good qualities and good things done in the past. Toast with water or milk, clicking glasses together. See that you don't toast one child more than another.

♥ 96 THE GIFTED CHILD

*O*ften a child who has very special talents or scores very high on tests is treated as if he is older than he really is. Remember to cuddle and love the gifted child just like the others. Don't let him think that his only value is a good mind. The gifted child needs to be reassured that he is accepted and loved for many more reasons than just his brilliance.

♥ 97 THE MORNING SQUEEZE

*A*t breakfast, hold hands around the table. Starting with a parent, send the message "I love you" around the table by squeezing the next hand three times. The next time around, squeeze four times for "Have a great day!" Then get going.

♥ 98 ALONE FOR AN HOUR

*W*hen a child is going to have to amuse herself alone for a period of time, prepare surprise activity cards. Make about ten cards, writing on each something the child would enjoy doing: read a book, teach Fido a trick, put a love note on Dad's pillow, make a new snack, listen to a record, play with a certain toy. Fold each card and staple it shut. Put them in a bowl on the table and tell her to pull one out whenever she's bored or lonely. When you return, talk about the activities she did.

♥ 99 WHO GETS THE CREDIT?

*P*arents aren't the only ones with good ideas. Make opportunities for kids to come up with good ideas. Then give credit where credit is due. Try to give that credit in front of others. This is especially important for a child who doesn't feel loved and appreciated.

♥ 100 TAKE A BOW

*P*art of growing up is participating in recitals. When your youngster is going to be in a recital, check with the teacher about the presentation of flowers. (It hurts when one child gets a bouquet and another

doesn't.) You may be put in charge of getting some sturdy flowers, wrapping the stems of each one with foil, and seeing that there is a presenter to hand one to each recitalist as he takes a bow.

♥ 101 THE BEST GIFT

*H*elping your child to understand that there is a God or Supreme Being on which he can rely, can be the greatest gift you give your child. Leaving a child spiritually bankrupt is actually a form of child abuse. Let your child know of God's loving care.

♥ 102 SILENT LOVE

*S*ometimes the best response to a youngster's problem is to just close your mouth! Parents often talk too much. When a child's feelings are hurt or he's suffered a great injustice, we don't need to question, rationalize, argue, suggest, or lay on soothing words. Just take the child into your arms and silently love him.

♥ 103 WAVING THE FLAG

*J*une is the month for Flag Day, but you don't have to wait until then to honor the flag. Learn the history and traditions of flag use (from the Scout handbook or the encyclopedia). Instill in your child a love for family and country. Let a child be in charge of putting up the flag each morning and taking it down at night. Talk about the pledge to the flag and what it means.

♥ 104 DISAPPEARING GRIPES

*L*ike magic, you can make petty gripes disappear. Just ask youngsters to write down the particulars of the gripe. They soon will see that some complaints aren't worth the time and trouble of finding pencil and paper and spelling out all those big words! When you do get a written complaint, be sure to put your arm around the child and say: "This must be very important to you, and thus it's very important to me."

♥ 105 FIRST RULES

*W*hen children are toddlers, start talking about family rules. These should cover crossing the street, playing with matches, coming when called, hitting and biting, eating snacks, and so forth. Write down

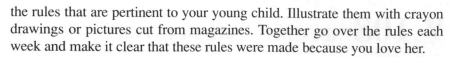

the rules that are pertinent to your young child. Illustrate them with crayon drawings or pictures cut from magazines. Together go over the rules each week and make it clear that these rules were made because you love her.

♥ 106 LET THEM DECIDE

A loving parent wants the best for his teen who will have to live within society's rules. Thus, the family rules are a good training ground. It's important to establish these rules before the teenage years come. When a child is about ten (or older if you didn't do this then) have a get-together to set new family guidelines. Let the kids share in making the rules and the all-important consequences of breaking them. Cover all those subjects that may cause problems in the years to come. Write them down, put them on the bulletin board so they won't be forgotten. And most important, once the rules are written, abide by them.

♥ 107 LET ME COUNT THE WAYS

W hen the whole family is together at supper, read aloud the poem "How Do I Love Thee?" (from *Sonnets from the Portuguese* by Elizabeth Barrett Browning). Talk about the various ways you love your children. You might even wish to write them down so they can be read by each child when he feels low.

♥ 108 SPECIAL MAIL DELIVERY

*E*veryone loves to get mail, so send a card to your child—right under your own roof. Don't use a stamp, just draw your own in the corner. Make or buy your card, or create it on computer.

♥ 109 SPECIAL MAIL DELIVERY— VALENTINE STYLE

*T*he day after Valentine's Day, during the usual half-price sale, one dad buys extra inexpensive valentines and uses them each month of the year. These love messages are happily received year-round.

♥ 110 "I SEE!"

*H*ere's the shortest and best way to react to some of the complaints, wild stories, and accusations that kids are always coming up with. With sincerity and enthusiasm just say "I see!" For, of course, you *do* see what is going on—and sometimes you don't need to get involved beyond "I see!" Sometimes saying that and adding a hug is all that is needed.

♥ 111 BECAUSE YOU LOVE THEM

*K*eep yourself in good health so you can meet your child's needs for a long time. Don't smoke, don't do drugs, don't drink and drive. And of course, set a good example by eating healthy foods.

♥ 112 HANDS ON

*W*hen life gets stressful, how about giving each other a back-scratch or back rub? End with three back-raps for "I love you."

♥ 113 HAPPY PILLOWCASE

*W*hen confined to bed, let a child create his own pillowcase. Use a tray covered with newspaper for a bed work-space. Put flat pages of newspaper inside the pillowcase to absorb any ink. On one side, let him use indelible marking pens to draw pictures and words. On the other side, let family members write loving get-well messages.

♥ 114 SHELF-PAPER BANNER

*F*or each child, cut a piece of paper about three feet long—shelf paper will do nicely. Tape a piece of stiff cardboard to each end, which will become the top and bottom. Tape a ribbon on the top as a hanger. Draw a heart in each corner. This banner is then personalized with the special qualities of each child. Start with a few and add others in the coming months. These might include: loving, honest, responsible, caring, sharing, helpful, funny, obedient, intelligent, kind, polite, diligent, athletic, musical, orderly, agreeable.

♥ 115 LONG-DISTANCE STORY TIME

*Y*ou can't always be home to read the bedtime story to a young child. Perhaps the grandparents live far away and never get that opportunity. Remedy this void by reading some favorite storybooks onto an audiocassette. Put a personalized "love and good night" message at the end.

♥ 116 WEAR A BOW, TAKE A BOW

*U*sed ribbon can be tied together into one big bow. A little child will like to wear it pinned to her shirt, on the back of her jeans, or in her hair. On a day when she's wearing the big bow, also show her how to take a bow. Each time she does something nicely, is helpful or loving, bow to each other. The ribbon bow shows creativity, the bowing of the body shows appreciation.

♥ 117 "I'M WILLING ..."

*F*riends and activities with friends are very important to teens. Be willing to encourage good times and good friends. (This may take some of your time, but it is easier than having to compete with bad influences.) Frequently use the phrase "I'm willing . . . ." Be willing to drive kids to events, to open your house and provide a place for a party, to share the family room, to chaperon an event. Be willing but not intrusive. Show your love by being willing to help your teen through these challenging years.

♥ 118 THE LOVE TREE

*O*n a special occasion such as a birthday, plant a tree in honor of the youngster. This can be in your backyard, or in connection with a project at a park or school. Let all the family help with the digging. See that the tree has proper care and watch it grow. Measure its height on the same day each year.

♥ 119 SLIP IT IN THE SLIPPER

*A*lmost every child under ten has a pair of beloved slippers. Use these as hiding places for love messages, a piece of wrapped candy, or a tiny gift. Don't do it routinely; do it only as a special surprise.

♥ 120 A TRUE LOVE STORY

♥ *LOVE ACROSS ALL BORDERS* ♥

*T*he cradle sat empty. Sometimes Wendy would rock it back and forth while stroking the pink fittings and the lonely teddy bear. She had been thinking about filling that cradle from the moment she became aware of abandoned baby girls in a faraway country, growing up in orphanages or dying from lack of care. The least she could do was save one little life. But how?

Her determination connected her with an adoption agency that helped her prepare the mountain of required documents and translations. And then came the wait. Finally, the wonderful day arrived when she was notified that a tiny baby girl had been assigned to her. Over and over she looked at the little face on the five-second video she'd received. Then came the scramble for clothes, formula, and supplies, and within weeks Wendy was off on a twenty-hour flight to a strange land where she knew no one. Gathering with other adoptive parents, an interpreter, and all their files and documents, they made their way into the countryside to the orphanage—no nurses or doctors, no running water, no one with time to hold or bathe or rock the babies.

The caregivers could not speak English, but announced the native name of each baby so that the parent could step forward and receive the child. Wendy was the last to be called forward, and when her baby's name was announced and the tiny child placed in her arms, she burst into

61

tears. The head of the orphanage assumed she didn't like the baby and, through the interpreter, offered to "trade her in" for another. But Wendy knew immediately that this was her long-awaited daughter.

Holding the baby was the thrilling part, but then the group embarked on weeks of frustrating bureaucratic paper-moving: signatures, permissions, payments, examinations, and obtaining official stamps on multiple copies, all the time caring for the babies in their small hotel rooms. When they went out to shop or eat, crowds gathered around the parents and babies and said, "America?" The parents nodded. The people smiled.

Their hopes were dashed one day when they were told that some important papers had been translated, but not by official translators. Perhaps they would not be able to adopt the babies after all. But the gloom changed into glory when the adoptions were mysteriously finalized. Now to leave the country before some official changed his mind.

After more paperwork, embassy visits, and exit examinations, they were finally given permission to leave. They had survived train trips, boat trips, small-plane trips, and at last they stepped on the jet for the long trip home. Now they were surrounded by family, friends, flowers, and gifts. Wendy and her daughter were home at last.

So, the cradle was no longer empty. It was filled with the daughter she had gone halfway around the world to bring home.

♥ 121 HIGH PRIORITY

*O*ccasionally cancel your own plans to do something your child thinks is important. Even if you're tired or busy, go to piano recitals, Little League ball games, or school plays. Show her that she has priority over almost anything. And definitely don't grumble about the time you spend.

♥ 122 CLIMBING KID

*L*et your crawling baby or toddler climb all over you as you sit or lie on the floor. Give a quick kiss when you can. Surprise him by rolling over. Turn your leg into a slide. Stand up and help him climb up your leg. Your body can be as good or better than any expensive piece of play equipment!

♥ 123 A REMINDER RIBBON

*W*hen you can't be with your child as much as you'd like, tie a gold ribbon (or one of her favorite color) on her wrist. Put it on the left wrist for a right-hander and vice versa. Tell her that the ribbon is her reminder that you will be thinking of her and loving her while you are separated.

♥ 124 SPEAK-LOVE DAY

*A*t breakfast on a day when the family will be together, announce that it is "Speak Love Day." This means that there will be no arguing, unkind criticism, hitting, meanness to babies or pets, insolence to parents, and so forth, for the entire day. Compliment good efforts. The idea may catch on—and wouldn't that be blissful!

♥ 125 "OUR BABY"

*W*hen there is a new member of the family, let an older child be the one to show off the baby. When relatives and friends visit, let your child hold the baby and tell what it is like to have a baby in the house. It helps an older sibling to accept and love the baby when the baby is "our baby" (the entire family's).

♥ 126 CHRISTMAS BIRTHDAYS

*S*ince one of our youngsters has a birthday near Christmas, we celebrate at the half-year point in June. In this way the birthday receives its proper importance, he has many more ideas on what gifts he might like, and our love and attention does not get lost in the holiday rush. Also, it alleviates the problem that many Christmas-birthday people talk of: someone giving you a gift and saying, "Happy Birthday and Merry Christmas."

♥ 127 FAILURE AND SUCCESS

*W*hen a child fails at something—a team loss, a bad grade, mistakes at the piano recital—her feeling of self-worth plummets. She may wonder how anyone could love such a loser. You can verbalize your loving care, and also help by immediately arranging for her to do something at which she excels.

♥ 128 TAMPERING WITH STORIES

*W*ith young children, you often read the same stories over and over. Make them more interesting by changing the text slightly. Change the name of one of the good characters to your child's name. Add sentences such as "He lived right on (your street name) and had a mama and daddy who loved him very much." If you have a pet, change the name of the animal in the story to your pet's name.

♥ 129 ARGUMENTATIVE QUESTIONS

*T*here's nothing that stifles family love more than constant arguments. Tell kids to ask themselves these questions *before* starting a quarrel: Does this make a real difference? Do I need to involve a parent in this? Is this the time to start and solve the dispute? Are there facts that would settle it? Even if I'm right, is it worth my time to argue? Can we just agree to disagree? Can we end this with a handshake or a hug?

♥ 130 ROCKER TIME

*T*here is something about a rocking chair that expresses love. If you don't have one, consider purchasing one or finding one at a garage sale. The rocker is where a parent comforts an infant, holds a toddler, reads to a young child, and where an older sister or brother can hold the

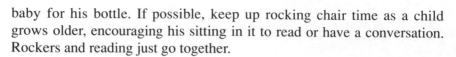

baby for his bottle. If possible, keep up rocking chair time as a child grows older, encouraging his sitting in it to read or have a conversation. Rockers and reading just go together.

♥ 131 HAVE I GOT NEWS FOR YOU!

*O*ften teens can be very placid and then suddenly very excited. Tune into those occasions when teens are bursting with news—even news you don't think is earth shattering. Still, listen intently and ask questions. Here is something that is important to them—thus it is important to you. Get the facts straight and ask if you can share the information with relatives and friends. Your teen will feel proud that you cared about his news.

♥ 132 LALA TIME

*I*n talking with your child, show your interest with LALA. This means: *Look* at the person and smile. *Ask* a question without prejudging. *Listen* carefully to what the person says. *Answer* all questions with kindness.

♥ 133 LULLABIES ARE BACK IN STYLE

*H*old a young baby close on your shoulder or in your lap and sing a lullaby while you slowly sway your body. When you softly sing a traditional song or a pop, country, or soft rock song, the soothing music helps a baby go to sleep. It doesn't matter if you can't remember all the words or if you don't have a voice for MTV, just sing a love song to your little one.

♥ 134 RAINBOW HEARTS

*M*ake up three boxes of gelatin—red, green, and yellow—and gel each different color in a separate flat pan. When firm, cut with a large heart-shaped cutter or knife. "Draw" with aerosol whipped cream "I ♥ U" on top. Serve several of each color on a plate for dessert or snack. All the pieces left over from cutting out the hearts can be diced and put in clear bowls for a pretty dessert the next day.

♥ 135 GIVING IS LOVING

*R*ather than emphasizing "What's in it for me?" teach children that giving to others is a form of loving. When a youngster is going off to an event, we usually say, "Go and have a good time." How much better to say, "Go and *give* a good time."

♥ 136 BELLRINGER

*S*ometimes when a child is ill and must stay in bed, she may feel abandoned and unloved. Supply her with a big bell to ring when she needs attention. This gives a child a feeling of security when you aren't with her, and it also helps her connect with the family.

♥ 137 MOTHER'S DAY

*W*hen children are young, it's dad's job to help prepare this special day. Homemade cards can express love and appreciation for a lot less money than purchased ones (and will be ever-so-much appreciated). Let this be a no-kitchen day for mom—others should make the meal and clean up afterward. A picnic in the park is a good way to spend the day because there are activities for all, so no one gets bored. A gift might be a plant for her desk at work, a new jogging shirt, tickets for a special event.

♥ 138 FATHER'S DAY

*U*ntil kids are old enough to plan this holiday on their own, mom has to help. Try a long banner (made on butcher paper or shelf paper) with an appropriate message and tack it up in a special place before dad wakes up. Consider serving a big breakfast in bed. Some families "kidnap" dad for the day and take him fishing, to the movies, or some special place he likes. (Just let him sit in the back of the car blindfolded and wonder where he's going!) Good gifts are books, golf or tennis balls, bright socks, a new tool—but no ties, please.

♥ 139 THREE LITTLE WORDS

While "I love you" are three great little words, there's another trio to learn: "I am sorry." When we truly care about one another, we want to apologize when we've hurt them. With kid help, make up some situations: when you bump into someone, when you're late, when you break something, when you forget. Practice saying "I am sorry." Then practice "I forgive you" and "I love you anyway."

♥ 140 SUITABLE SNACKS

You love your child too much to let him "pig out" on the wrong foods. But, you don't like being the ogre and always saying *no* to snacks. With the help of your youngsters, find some munchy that is nutritious: raisins, crunchy cereal, low calorie sugar-free cookies, small crackers, trail mix. Then, make a snack container out of a one-quart plastic jar with a tight lid. Label the container for each child, such as: Chris's No-Need-to-Ask Snacks. Fill it up only once a week so the snacker learns to be responsible for his intake.

♥ **141** HOLDING HANDS IN CEMENT

*F*ind a place in your backyard where you could use a large stepping stone. Level the area and put wood strips around the edges. Using bags of ready-to-mix cement, fill in the space. Wait until the cement begins to set up. With the family gathered around on all sides, let each one press a hand into the cement, just touching the end finger of the preceding hand, forming a circle of love. Have plenty of newspaper on hand to wipe off the hands. You can carve names around the outside edge if you wish.

♥ **142** ADMIT MISTAKES, OR COVER UP?

*T*he words *I was wrong* or *I made a mistake* are difficult to say—so treat them that way. When a child admits a transgression, pour on the love. Make it easy to tell the truth. If punishment is needed, make it lighter than if there had been a cover-up. And don't forget to admit your own parental blunders. Don't let kids think you never err. You'll find that the parent/child relationship is much smoother when both sides are truthful.

♥ **143** BE MY GUEST

*E*veryone loves a pleasant guest, so show your children the necessary manners before going to social events. These include: expressing interest in other guests, including loners in activities, contributing to the conversation, being willing to try new foods or new games, helping set up or clean up after the event, enthusiastically thanking for gifts, telling the host or hostess how much you enjoyed the event.

♥ 144 HAVE A LAUGH-IN

*A*ppreciate humor at your house. Share stories of funny things that happen. Then, retell them. Tell jokes. If you need a start, borrow joke books from the library or buy a joke-a-day calendar. Laugh at yourself when you do something silly. Remember the old Swedish proverb: Laughter lives in the same house as love.

♥ 145 PICKY EATERS

*S*ome kids play with their food, turning it into designs, stacks, or mush with very little ending up in the mouth. You can often encourage better eating habits and good nutrition by making meals more inviting. For example, there's more to breakfast than eggs, toast, or cereal. Try a fruit shake and peanut butter on toast. As an alternative to the lunchtime sandwich, consider a stuffed tomato with crackers and cheese. For dinner, let the vegetables be dunked in a variety of dips. Read *Feed Me! I'm Yours* (Vicki Lansky, Bantam Books, 1974)—an old but good book.

♥ 146 LOVE ANGELS

*A*sk your child to help you make some simple three-dimensional angels out of white tissue paper. Fold one sheet in half and then fold down the top four inches. Put tape or a rubber band around this fold at the three-inch mark, to make the neck. Fluff to make a head and draw on eyes and mouth. Spread the bottom to make the body. To make the wings, take a second sheet, folded in half and in half again. Squeeze it together in the middle. Taper the ends of the wings with scissors. Tape to the back. Spread the wings. With thread, hang from the ceiling over his bed. Give names to the angels. Let one be the Mamma Angel and one the Papa Angel. Tell your child that God's angels are always loving him, and watching over him.

♥ 147 NICKNAME FUN

*T*alk about the names and nicknames of each family member. Tell how you chose each child's name. Ask what each person would rename herself if she had the opportunity. With a name book, look up the old meanings of your names. Talk about the pet names you used when the children were little—those cute names that expressed how much you loved them.

♥ 148 PATIENT LOVE

*I*t's so exciting when a youngster begins to talk. And so frustrating when you can't understand everything he's saying. Patiently repeat the words you understand (hearing the words spoken correctly will teach him to speak clearly) and then repeat the words or sounds that you don't understand. With great love and tenderness in your voice, ask him to repeat the words so you can understand. Your consideration will be reflected in his willingness to try to communicate clearly. Urgent demands on his part become less urgent when you sit down with a child and try to understand what he wants. This procedure takes patient love, but you will be rewarded with a better speaking and acting toddler.

♥ 149 CHRISTMAS IN JULY?

*M*ade-up holidays arc fun for the family and show how much you care about building loving memories. Have a "five months to Christmas" party on July 25. Bring out a few Christmas decorations, put up the train and play with it, make a batch of Christmas cookies, exchange silly little gifts, play Christmas carols on the stereo, have a small turkey with all the trimmings. And, it isn't too soon to start those Christmas wish lists!

♥ 150 COMPLAINT DEPARTMENT

*T*his doesn't sound like a love session, but that's often the end result. When friction builds up and love flies out the window, have a family meeting. Let all family members air their complaints without judging or interrupting. Then consider the complaints one at a time, calmly looking for underlying causes, and possible conclusions. Everyone should shake hands when the complaint session is over.

♥ 151 THE AMAZING MAZE

*H*ere's an idea that will be sure to bring smiles and hugs. Collect many large sturdy boxes (twelve or more), large enough for a child to crawl through. Cut an opening on two sides of each, sometimes on adjacent sides, sometimes on opposite sides. Make billboards on the inside: "All the world loves Alan," "Elsie is funny," "Dad wants a hug." Lay out the boxes on the floor of a large room, in the yard, or in the garage—anywhere children can play for many days. Don't put them in a straight line, but rather make some turns. Make a "dead end" along the way, forcing the crawler to back up and choose another route. Using heavy sealing tape, tape the boxes together. Now, let the kids crawl through or have races to see who can go through the fastest.

♥ 152 THE LOVE CIRCLE

*F*irst thing in the morning, last thing at night, in the dark when camping out, just before someone leaves on a trip—any time can be a good time for a "Love Circle." Stand close in a circle, putting your hands behind those on either side of you, and grasp the hands of the persons one away from you (not next to you). This weaves the group together. Then move forward to be ever closer, or move back as far as you can, stand on tiptoe, go 'round and 'round, sit on the ground, but don't let go.

♥ 153 PART OF THE GOOD GANG

A lonely child can find friends in after-school activities, sports, and groups such as Camp Fire and Scouts. But, the group must be of the child's choosing. Sometimes lonely children don't want to be in any group where they might risk rejection, so you might give a child a choice of group activities and encourage her to try just one for a specified limited time. Shyness is eased if you can have the group meet at your house, or carpool to games, or ask a fellow scout to come over for play or dinner. A loving parent will not let loneliness go unnoticed.

♥ 154 TERMS OF ENDEARMENT

*T*here are many little love-names that you can share with a little child. See which ones she likes, and let her use some for you. Consider: honey-bun, dearie, cutie baby, love-bug, darling, little one, bunnykins, doll, huggy-bear, sweetheart, sweetie-pie.

♥ 155 HURRY, HURRY?

*A*re you always rushing your children to get ready, finish eating, get to bed? Do you feed, clothe and bathe your baby hurriedly? If so, you are sending a hidden message that you don't have time enough to enjoy and love your child—that your work and other activities are more important than he is. Slow down . . . and give a loving message. Childhood goes by so quickly!

♥ 156 LOVE TIME

*W*hen children are to be separated from you, choose a special time for each of you to send loving thoughts to one another. Call it "Love Time." Decide together on a convenient time in the morning, during the lunch hour, or just before bed as your quiet communication time to send love across the miles.

♥ **157** AVOID THE BIG *IF*

*D*on't just express love on those occasions when your child pleases you. You don't want a child to think that you only love him IF he is obedient or IF he doesn't wet the bed, or IF he finishes his dinner. When your child makes a mistake, tell him how much you love him and want to help him.

♥ **158** VELCRO FLAG

*O*n a rainy or boring day, work with the kids to make this family flag to hang on a hall wall or at the front door. Use a fabric at least three-by-five feet wide. Put squares of Velcro on it so you can decorate it with Velcro-backed messages (or take the easy route and use pins to affix the messages). Using fabric marking pens on plain fabric, make up a variety of messages that include family names, numbers (for ages), and achievements such as graduation, birthday, first communion, making the team, and so forth. In this way your banner can say: "Whitney is eight" or "Matt made the team" or "Kristin graduates." Kids will feel loved for the special recognition.

♥ 159 MONEY VERSUS A GIFT

*M*any grandparents give up on what to give teens and just give money. While money is always welcome, gifts can show special interest. However, this means that a grandparent needs to know the teen's needs and likes. This can be achieved by asking him for a wish list, or conferring with the parents. One wise grandma knows that it's fun to get both gifts and cash. So, it's her practice to give a small gift and tie a balloon to it. Inside the balloon she's put some rolled up bills, her "love money." (This is easy to do if you insert the rolled up bills into the neck of the balloon before blowing it up.)

♥ 160 WAITING FOR WONDERS?

*S*ome parents wait until something praiseworthy happens to say something encouraging to their kids. Enjoy and appreciate your child "as is" by praising the little things during the day: the cheerful way he went off to school, the way he patted the dog, the way he let his friend have the bigger truck for play, the way he didn't complain at bedtime. Look for these everyday wonders and then show you care.

♥ 161 SEATTLE HUG

*T*each this when children are young and keep it up for all the years to come. It's a good way to hug such people as aunties, brothers, and ladies at church. (It was invented at a teen meeting in Seattle.) When affectionately greeting someone, take these four steps: (1) Face the person and smile. (2) Take hold of the upper arms (that way you can control how close you get). (3) To avoid noses meeting, go to the right of the other person's face. (4) Brush cheeks or give a light kiss. It's friendly, easy to do, and you'll even get your preteen son to hug Auntie Beatrice this way!

♥ 162 DISCOURAGING DISCOURAGEMENT

*S*ome youngsters seem to wallow in misery—although inwardly they hate it. They say things like, "I'll never get this done," or "I'm not as smart as Michelle," or "I'm always the one on the bench." Tell your youngster that even champions feel discouraged sometimes. Many great people sat on the bench. The important thing is to keep pursuing your dream, to pay attention to the game of life, to be a player and not a specta-tor. When a child makes statements that show discouragement, be alert to the hurt. Acknowledge his emotions as a *temporary* loser. Identify his feelings of annoyance, pressure, and fear. Listening and understanding are important. Only then talk about the winning situations he has been in. "Do you remember when . . . ." statements will help and encourage.

♥ 163 A LOVING RESOURCE

*D*on't overlook grandparents and other relatives and friends as wonderful and loving resources. Don't just use them to babysit. Encour-age good communication between the generations through visits, sharing of skills, learning family history, and as surrogate parents at sporting

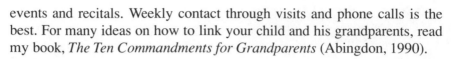

events and recitals. Weekly contact through visits and phone calls is the best. For many ideas on how to link your child and his grandparents, read my book, *The Ten Commandments for Grandparents* (Abingdon, 1990).

♥ 164 BEING A KID

*T*here are too few years of childhood, so love your kid by letting her be a kid. Maturing doesn't come overnight (in fact at times you think it will never come!). It arrives little by little as you teach skills, good habits, appropriate behavior. Childish behavior isn't something to be derided—it's normal. Yes, your child *will* grow up—all it takes is time and patience.

♥ 165 ALOHA SANDWICH

*T*ry this Hawaiian way of holding hands. Each person places his or her hand atop another's, making a big stack of touching hands, and eventually using both hands of each participant. Then the bottom hand is pulled out and placed on top, and so forth, making the "sandwich." This pulls you close together.

♥ 166 LOVE, WHEN A RELATIVE DIES

*W*ith your youngster, look at a scrapbook or photo album containing pictures of the relative. Talk about good times you all had in the past and some of the achievements of that person. A young child may want to draw a picture of the two of them enjoying an activity. An older child may want to write down a memorable experience to share with other relatives. Be sure to give kids of all ages extra attention and love at such times.

♥ 167 GLORIA'S GATE

*G*randma Gloria is a hugger. She loves to sit on the floor and then invites her little grandson to come "in the gate" for a hug. She makes the "gate" with her arms and legs. Wearing slacks, she spreads her legs out in a wide V, and does the same with her arms. When he comes in the "gate," she closes her arms and legs and holds him tightly. When he says, "Open the gate," she does so and he runs out, but she finds that he usually wants to come back in for a second hug.

♥ 168 PROBLEM SOLVING

*A*s much as we want solutions to our challenges, problem *solving* is a topic we often dread. But, it's important to teach youngsters some problem-solving techniques. Consider borrowing a library book on the subject. But most important, remember to praise a child for her ingenuity: "It's amazing how you did that!" "How clever you are to have thought of that solution." "I never would have come up with such a good idea." "I'm proud of your good thinking."

♥ **169** AFTER YOU'VE GONE

*S*ometimes parting is sad. A parent goes on a business trip, relatives leave after a visit, a friend moves away, an older sibling marries or moves into her own place. The void left can be partly filled with a short note left by the person leaving. Hide it under a pillow or in a frequently used drawer. One grandpa always hides a granola bar in his grandson's sock drawer with a note like "Can't wait to see you next time. Love, Gramps." An uncle doesn't write a message, he just leaves a silver dollar in a child's shoe as a reminder of his love.

♥ **170** LUNCH-BOX LOVE

*A*dd surprises to the lunch box: a cartoon or comic strip, a small puzzle, a love message inside the paper napkin (or on it), a smile carved into the apple skin, a little person made of marshmallows and gum drops.

♥ 171 SAYING *NO*

*S*tart when children are young to gently discipline them. Don't hesitate to use the word *no* with a baby. Don't bury the word in a sentence such as "Daddy doesn't really want you to do that, so he's saying no to you, little darling." Keep it simple. Other ways of showing right from wrong are removing a child to a different location when she is angry or antagonistic, firmly removing a child from something that shouldn't be touched, turning your back on a child who is displaying unacceptable behavior. You love your child too much to let him be a terrorizing toddler.

♥ 172 CAMP LOVE

*A*lthough most kids are eager to go away to camp, many find that they get homesick once they are there. Let a child take along a small picture of the family. Write some cheerful and encouraging messages— just a line or two—seal them in small envelopes, and suggest the youngster open one of these when he gets lonely. Give the camper a diary or small notebook in which to make notes of his experience to share at his homecoming celebration dinner.

♥ 173 A MEMORY OF LOVE

*W*e can help a child build a storehouse of wonderful memories. When there is a special event, such as a wedding or party, a championship game, or a special sunset at the lake, take a quiet moment to think about it. After the event or before leaving the lake, take a "memory moment" with your child. Shut your eyes and visualize the scene in thought. Commit it to memory in this way. You can certainly take a photo, but by keeping special pictures in thought, they are always with you. They don't take up space and they never fade. Remember to look at your child each morning and hold that loving face in your own memory.

♥ 174 MATCHING FUNDS

*T*eens have many financial needs and wants—a first car, prom clothes, college funds. Grandparents can sometimes help by providing matching funds. For example, if the youngster earns half the money, the grandparent will then pay the other half. Some families start an education fund when a child is young and then keep it growing. Parents can also match contributions the youngster makes from job earnings.

♥ 175 STICKER LOVE

*G*et a supply of stickers with hearts or smiles on them. Use them to recognize a good school paper brought home, or chores completed. Have some larger ones to use for very special achievements.

♥ 176 THAT FIRST DAY APART

*W*hen a young child leaves home for the first time, put a reminder of love in her pocket. This could be a penny, a large paper clip, a pretty hankie, a little pencil. Tell the child that this is a reminder of your love, and, without anyone else knowing, she can slip her hand in her pocket and remember that you're thinking about her and loving her.

♥ 177 GOT AN ATTITUDE?

*N*owadays most everyone is tuned in to attitudes. We're beginning to recognize where we come from and how we react because of these inner feelings. Take time with your family to talk about important positive attitudes and how you can cultivate the best of them: a loving attitude, a determined attitude, a teachable attitude, a positive mental attitude. Also discuss detrimental attitudes (defeatist, destructive, negative, self-pitying). When you see some of these bad atttitudes surfacing, work diligently to help the child change them. Above all, while a child is going through a negative time, be especially loving.

♥ 178 DAD'S LUNCH

*T*here is something magical about going to lunch with dad, and when a child is feeling lonely, this can be a real pepper-upper. A child can ask one or two acquaintances (from school, church, or the neighborhood) to go along. This is an opportunity to get to know one another and also a time when a dad can subtly direct the conversation to a topic that *his child* enjoys and would be interesting to the friends. For example, the dad could say, "My son really likes HO-gauge trains. Maybe you can stop on the way home to see one he has set up." Don't push, but sometimes a parent needs to manufacture friend-making opportunities.

♥ 179 AWARD NIGHT

*A*ppreciation is needed when kids do chores around the house. But first, you have to help kids to do those chores. Change jobs each month, letting children be sidewalk sweeper, kitchen helper, bathroom cleaner, wastebasket emptier, or whatever jobs aid you the most. Provide a chart so the chores can be checked off as completed each day—that way you don't have to nag. If a child has four chores to do each day, his score for the month should be 112 or 124 check marks, depending on how many days are in the month. Near the end of the month, take the chart down and keep it hidden as you (rather than the kids) record the chores completed. On the last day of the month, have Award Night at dinner. Announce the new chores schedule for the coming month, and then, with fanfare, present a framed award with ribbons on it or a special crown to the helper with the highest score.

♥ **180** A TRUE LOVE STORY

♥ *TOUGH LOVE WINS* ♥

*B*arry couldn't believe it—Monica wanted him to have custody of their thirteen-year-old daughter, Allison! Monica's new job involved extended travel and she felt Barry could better manage a young teenager. After all, Allison was a "good girl" and Barry's job was of the nine-to-five variety so he could be an attentive dad mornings and evenings.

He'd always thought that being a parent wasn't too difficult. Besides, during the separation that preceded their divorce, Monica had moved out of the old house, taking Allison and forcing Barry to improve his home-making talents. Now, Allison would move back in and they'd be a happy twosome. Yes, this was going to be okay.

Early in the evening when Monica brought Allison back home and told them good-bye, she said to Barry, "Ask her about school." Barry thought that Allison would share some happy story about academic achievement, so he prepared dishes of ice cream with peaches and whipped cream, and the two sat down on the back porch in the semi-darkness. Barry gave a sigh of well-being and dutifully asked, "Well, what's new at school?"

Allison looked into her bowl, toyed with the melting ice cream, and softly said, "I've been expelled." And so the whole story tumbled out: her depression during the year of separation and divorce, a new friend who had access to unlimited liquor, the daily after-school drinking bouts, arguments with her mother, liquor parties off campus during lunchtime, the outburst in the classroom when a teacher suggested she had been drinking, and finally the shoving session with the principal who then expelled her. Silence.

Now it was Barry's turn to look down into his melting ice cream. This was a thirteen-year-old, his own sweet baby daughter. How could this be? He wanted to scream for Monica, but he knew she couldn't help. He choked out the words, "Where do we go from here?"

Allison looked startled. "Don't you want to shout at me?"

He replied, "Sure, but that wouldn't help us figure this out—together."

The next morning, despite the press of office work, Barry took Allison to visit the principal, who referred them to a counselor, who referred them to a group for teen alcoholics. Barry felt encouraged when Allison agreed to go to meetings and was accepted back in school. "Ah," he thought, "I've done it, we're through this."

Early one afternoon a few months later, he stopped at the house en route to a meeting. There, right in his living room, was the noise of MTV, potato chips on the floor, two bottles and five cans, and three very drunk teens sprawled amid the potato chips.

Barry prepared himself for the challenge of his lifetime—a time for tough love. That very night, when Allison could sullenly comprehend his words, he set down new rules: He would drive her to school each morning, he was cutting off all her money, he took her house key, he was revoking the permission to leave campus at lunch—she would carry lunch from home, he would arrange for an after-school club activity, he'd pick her up before dinner, and he would go with her to her group support session twice weekly.

But most important, he talked to Allison more, told her how much he loved her, helped her find new friends and activities, and promised a special summer if she stayed sober. There were times they had fierce arguments, but he remained tough and let the rules with preset punishments rule the house. Sometimes the only thing he could do was hold her and kiss away the tears.

It took two years, but Barry and Allison finally won. She graduated from high school with top honors and set a bold example of "no alcohol for me" at college. And a few years after college, when she and her husband had their first baby, she named the boy Barry in honor of the man who had saved her life.

♥ 181 GET SMART

*I*f you feel your parenting skills could be improved, take a class or read some books. Join a neighborhood parent group. Being with other parents will give you information and encouragement—and you won't feel your problems are unique, but instead solvable. Being the best parent you can be is one more way of showing your love.

♥ 182 OH, THOSE ASHTRAYS!

*N*ow that smoking is no longer politically correct, the clay projects brought home from school are likely to be mugs and bowls instead of the formerly popular ashtrays. Well, whatever the product, parents should give it applause! Display it on the coffee table (other parents will admire your taste) and use it, if possible. Later, it can be stored in the child's own memory box.

♥ 183 OH, THOSE DRAWINGS!

*G*reat masterpieces of art come home from school almost every week. Some get hung on the refrigerator, some on the wall, but what happens later? Don't sneak this art into the rubbish! Ask a child if he would like it kept. If so, put the picture in a special drawer for later inclusion in the family scrapbook. This shows you appreciate your child's work, and who knows, he may grow up to be a famous artist!

♥ 184 THE SCRAPBOOK DRAWER

*E*very house needs a place to store memorabilia, like those special pictures kids bring home from school. Establish a drawer for just such things as well as programs, postcards, awards, photos, clippings— the mementoes of happy times together. (At the end of each month, put a large piece of paper into the drawer to keep the items separated by month.) Once a year, perhaps on New Year's Day, put all these items into a scrapbook. Let kids help by gluing in items or making marking pen comments. Leave it out where family and friends can enjoy it as a tangible memory of the good things that happened during the year.

♥ 185 WHAT WAS YOUR INTENTION?

*S*ome of the biggest in-house disasters come from a child's wish to do something nice, and you shouldn't get angry if the motive was a good one. (One of our kids wedged flowers between each of the piano keys to show his love.) Much, much later you may want to suggest a better way, but for the present, show your appreciation of the love and give love back. When Susie uses all your shaving cream to spray a "Happy Birthday, Daddy" message on the mirror, keep your sense of humor.

♥ 186 MY LIFE

*B*edtime stories don't have to be from storybooks—some of the best are right inside your head. You may not be a famous author, but you have had many years of living, so choose episodes from your own life to use as bedtime stories. Kids will be amazed at some of the adventuresome things you've done.

♥ **187** BUILD A FORT

*W*hen a child is ill and has to stay in bed, make the time pleasant. Make some balls out of tissue or newspaper. Show the child how to build a fort right in bed using the blankets and pillows to make a barrier in the middle of the bed. The child sits or lies behind his fort. You sit on the other side. Throw the balls at the child and give him a love message with each one, such as "I love you when you're sick or well." Or, "I'm here to love and care for you." Prepare for him to throw the balls back at you. You know he's feeling better when he scores a solid hit.

♥ **188** LISTENING BETWEEN THE LINES

*W*e need to really listen to a child—not just what she is saying, but also what she is saying "between the lines." Along with her enthusiasm for an accomplishment may be regret over how much time it took to the detriment of her social life. Behind the comment that a friend is mean may be a request for *your* love. Along with a plea to stay home from some school event may be a fear about shyness, appearance, or social graces. Be understanding and loving, and try to discuss the real need.

♥ 189 SIGNALS OF LOVE

*S*ometimes words aren't possible. Instead, use a sign of love as a child leaves the car pool or comes up to bat, or goes out the door with friends to play. Try these signals: thumbs up, a wink, index finger and thumb making a circle for O.K., two hands together as if in prayer, one hand up as in a "high five," a high kick. Let kids tell you which signal they like best.

♥ 190 STAYING HOME FROM SCHOOL

*I*t doesn't show love for your own child—or others in the class-room—if you send a sick youngster to school. However, there are times when a child doesn't seem to have an illness, but complains about not feeling well and asks to stay home. If circumstances permit, let there be one—only one—quiet day at home while zeroing in on the problem. Let that day be *quiet* with reading, napping and doing any homework—not a day of television, outside play, or errands with you. During that one day, find a clear reason and take care of the problem. A wise mother who used this method says it does away with parent/child wrangling, and usu-ally the child was back in school the next day.

♥ 191 ART APPRECIATION

*W*hen a child has drawn a picture, ask her permission to take it to your office where you can tape it on the wall and show it to your co-workers. Tell her that it will be a during-the-day reminder of how much you love and appreciate her.

♥ 192 ARF AND MEOW

*D*ogs and cats, as well as birds, fish and hamsters, have feelings. Talk about how a pet might feel if neglected, not talked to, fed, or played with. Giving regular care is one way we show love. At first, help youngsters to care for their pets and then expect them to follow through. Be aware of the feeding and care until you're sure the pet isn't being neglected. Take pictures of pets and their owners cuddling together (unless it's a goldfish!).

♥ 193 THE RIGHT TITLE

*R*ather than the words "the fourth of July," give the proper title: Independence Day. Talk about the meaning of the holiday and how it got started. Have your own parade and ask everyone on your street to participate. Decorate bikes, wagons, wheelchairs, strollers, and cars.

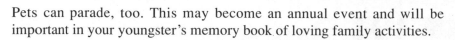

Pets can parade, too. This may become an annual event and will be important in your youngster's memory book of loving family activities.

♥ 194 RILY

*T*his is an acronym for "Remember I Love You." Put it on notes and letters or say it over the phone or as kids go off to school or play. Encourage kids to use it when they may not feel comfortable using the actual words. Have them check to see if good friends and relatives know the secret meaning of RILY.

♥ 195 ABRAHAM'S STORY

*I*f a child feels discouraged or unappreciated, tell her about Abraham. He dropped out of grade school. He went broke running a little store. He was in debt for fifteen years. He had an unhappy marriage. He ran for the House and lost twice. He ran for the Senate and lost twice. He gave a great speech at Gettysburg, but the audience was apathetic. The newspapers attacked him daily. Half of the country despised him. Yet this awkward, rumpled, brooding man inspired the world. His name was Abraham Lincoln.

♥ **196** SIGN LOVE

*T*each children the international hand sign for "I love you." Raise the right hand, palm outward, and lower the middle two fingers. The thumb, index finger, and little finger remain upward. Sign "love" as kids leave for school or as you catch their eye out on the playground.

♥ **197** WHAT DO YOU HAVE IN MIND?

*M*ost parents are diligent in keeping their youngsters' bodies free from poisons, bad influences and habits, and contagion. Yet, they are not as caring as to what goes into a child's consciousness. What is taken into a child's mind (from violent television or movies, from poisonous theories that try to control a child's thinking and acting) can be far more damaging. Show your love by being protective of what your youngster takes into *both* body and mind.

♥ **198** A COMPLIMENTARY DINNER

*O*ne day each month or so, have a supper where everyone tries to go overboard with compliments. Some will be sincere, some overdone, some just funny, but everyone will feel good. These compliments can range from "How majestic you look," and "You're eating so neatly that the ants under the table will starve," to "These cookies are so incredibly delicious we should send them to the President" and "This hamburger is better than filet mignon."

♥ **199** GRATEFUL GRACE

*S*ome families give thanks to God before a meal, and often in an effort to get to the food, the words are routine and rapid. Talk about the importance of appreciating the good that has come to us. Take turns giving a brief grace that expresses love and gratitude to God, and appreciation for family members and friends. A child going on a trip or about to be in the school play will be comforted by a prayer that specifically mentions him.

♥ **200** QUESTION TIME WITH TEENS

*W*hen riding in the car or sprawled on the sofa, start a conversation on love. Here are some questions to consider:

How does a parent best show love to a teenager?
How does a teen best show love to a parent?
What are ways to show appreciation?
How can you put aside the hurts of the past?
When someone is mean, how can you react with love?
What's the difference between family love and boy/girl love?
Should we love the unlovable? If so, how?
How can parents and teens express love when they're separated?

♥ 201 AND I'M AN ELEPHANT

*S*ometimes kids say totally impossible things because they are discouraged or hurt or need attention. Things like: "I'm the ugliest person in the world," or "I'll never understand geometry in a thousand years." While you will sometimes want to reason with them about an absurd statement, sometimes you can make the same point with an equally preposterous one, such as "And I'm an elephant."

♥ 202 ONE ON ONE

*S*ometimes parents don't have enough time alone with each child. When ours were teens and preteens, we arranged a special day each month to do what that child wanted—just one parent and one child. I went bowling with one son, to the mall "just to look" with a daughter, to art galleries and museums with another son. Your child may want to go to the beach with you, or out to breakfast, or to a game or a play. It's their choice, and you'll get to know more about your youngsters' interests. Certainly it takes up a block of your time, but it shows your caring love.

♥ 203 CHECKING UP

*S*ometimes a little child feels lonely or afraid when going to bed. After you've said "I love you," also say "and I'll be checking on you as you fall asleep." It is very reassuring to a child to know that someone is looking in on him. And, of course, be sure to do so.

♥ 204 TURN SAD INTO GLAD

*S*o often Labor Day is a depressing holiday for the kids, signaling the end of summer vacation and the start of school. Make it a special day, honoring both work and play. Decide on one large labor project for the morning (fence painting or garage cleaning). While working, talk about labor and the kind of work your kids might enjoy as a profession, and also about unions and trade associations. Then celebrate the remainder of the day with an activity that the kids really enjoy.

♥ 205 SCHOOL-SUPPLIES MESSAGES

*O*ften parents have to buy supplies for school projects. These might be a brush, marker, special paper, a notebook, or craft supplies. When you've bought such items, don't just leave them in the child's room. Put a little love message with them, something like "I can't wait to see what you'll do with this. Love, Pops." It's just one more opportunity to show you care about your youngster and his education.

♥ 206 HOW DOES IT FEEL?

*W*hen a child is thoughtless, teach her to be more loving in this way: Ask her "How does it feel . . . ?" How does it feel to be hit, to be ignored, to be called names, to find that someone forgot something important to you, to have someone steal from you, to be lied to. Turning the tables is a good way to teach.

♥ 207 A PLEDGE FOR KIDS

*B*ecause you love your children and want them to have a good life, encourage them to take this pledge (copy it and have them sign it):

"I realize that the greatest power in the world is the power of knowledge. I want to be smart because misinformed people miss many rewards. I will learn my basic skills and be expert in them. I will read books on subjects that interest me, but I'll also read on other subjects to make me aware of the world around me. I will discuss at dinnertime what I've learned at school today. I will study our nation's history and see how these ideas can help me today. I will set aside time to think about my future and talk over ideas that can guarantee that future. I pledge this to those who love me and are trying to help me succeed. More important, I pledge it to myself."

(This pledge is an adaptation of a *Wall Street Journal* ad by United Technologies Corporation.)

♥ **208** A PLEDGE FOR PARENTS

*A*s a companion to the preceding pledge, this parent's pledge was also printed by United Technologies. It too echoes a parent's love in seeing that the child has a good education.

"I want my child to have the best possible education and I realize that strong school systems are essential. I will provide a home environment that will encourage my child to learn. I will help my child build a meaningful home library. I will not do my child's homework but I will insist that homework assignments be completed on time. I will discuss at dinnertime what my child has learned at school that day. I will include stimulating books among the gifts I give my child. I will review newspaper stories and TV newscasts with my child and discuss how these affect our lives. I will be in regular contact with my child's teachers. I will remind my child of the necessity of discipline in the classroom—especially self-discipline. I will help my child appreciate and enjoy the excitement of learning and the joys of an inquiring mind."
(The parent can sign this and give it to the child.)

♥ **209** CHILD-HEALTH DAY

*T*his is usually observed the first Monday of October. During the long summer, some families slip into careless eating habits. Have a family discussion on good nutrition and fitness. Include some remarks about your own shortcomings and goals. Tell children you love them too much to let them fall into bad health habits. Decide on several improvements you can all make and post a list of them on the bulletin board or refrigerator. Review your good intentions each month and see how you're doing.

♥ 210 PEEK-A-BOO

*L*ittle children associate this game with happy play. Use it at crying times, too, and bring back the smiles. When a child is crying, put your hands over her eyes, then take them away quickly, then put your hands back, and so forth. Say "I see a crying Susie, I see a happy Susie." You can also do this by covering your own eyes and pretending to cry and then laugh.

♥ 211 NEW-HORIZONS DAY

*E*ach year in August, before school starts, meet with each child separately to discuss her educational progress, financial needs, and especially how satisfied and happy she is with her life. Tell her how much you appreciate what she's done during the past year. Emphasize your love and trust. This is a good time to set a new later bedtime (even if just ten or fifteen minutes), to increase her allowance, to decide what new clothes are needed for school, and to talk about upcoming after-school activities. Encourage her hopes and assure her that you'll do all you can to help her make them happen.

♥ 212 s.o.

*I*n the theater or the ball park, this means "standing ovation." Everyone rises and applauds the star. At home it works best when a child needs extra love and appreciation. Save this for special achievements, but on those occasions encourage everyone in the room to rise and applaud.

♥ 213 DISPELLING TANTRUMS

*W*hile most tantrums are scary and annoying for parents, they are also scary for the child. However, they are not unusual in toddlerhood. The first things to do are: take a deep breath, be sure that it is not a seizure or other physical problem, and see that the child is in a safe place where he can kick or thrash. Some tantrums will fade away on their own; others require some parent action. Sometimes just holding a child and telling him that you love him and that everything will be okay is sufficient. Other times, a music box or cassette may soothe. Try going out on the grass and lying down together where you can both kick and shout. (This may surprise him and he'll stop to watch you.) Putting a child's hands in *cool* running water may stop the screaming. And if it seems the child is seeking attention this way, you can just turn your back and not look at him. Depriving him of attention may quiet him down. When the tantrum is over, express a lot of love. If the child experiences many tantrums, read up on them in child-care books and consider getting professional help.

♥ 214 WHIRL AROUND

*S*coop up your toddler by her armpits and whirl her through the air like a merry-go-round. Swing her high and low, and in and out from you while saying, "I love you when you're far from me, I love you when you're near to me."

♥ 215 WHICH FORK?

*E*tiquette isn't often taught at home nowadays, but you are giving a child a great gift if you teach basic manners. A youngster who is crude and uncouth is often unwelcome and shunned. Save your child this hurt by making good manners automatic—things such as table manners, party manners, introductions, writing thank-you notes, showing respect for elders.

♥ 216 PHOTO TREE

*O*btain photos of both sets of grandparents, you the parents, and your children. Paste them on a large piece of paper, one generation on each level, like a tree. Between each set of grandparents write: Grandpa Walt loves Grandma Alice, Grandpa Bob loves Grandma Elaine. On the parent level, do the same for yourself and your spouse. Then on the kid level write: Everybody loves (the children's names).

♥ 217 DON'T BE A QUITTER

*W*hen a child wants to give up and you want to be encouraging, tell him that anybody can give up. It takes no talent. And besides, it is just what the opposition hopes he'll do. If he really wants to continue, tell him you'll support him because you love him. Remind him that a man named Winston Churchill said, "Never give in. Never. Never!" He stuck his chin out and wouldn't give up when his country was losing a war. It took time, but he was eventually victorious. Your child can be, too.

♥ 218 THE UNBIRTHDAY CELEBRATION

*H*ave an unbirthday celebration for the entire family whenever you choose. Have party food (little sandwiches, chips, cupcakes) and play games. Or you may want to serve cake and ice cream to the children's friends. Such celebrations say "I care" and they make any day special.

♥ 219 LOVING WORDS

*H*elp children to use love words by setting an example. Say such things as: "I love to be helped." "I like what you are doing." "I love you all the time." "I care so much for you." "I loved being with you today." "You're fantastic." "You're special." "You're beautiful." "You're precious." "You mean the world to me." Make *love* a common word, so that kids aren't startled when you say it. Sometimes, too, you have to say, "I love you too much to let you do that."

♥ 220 PRAISING WORDS

*T*ry these phrases that give a youngster a sense of self-worth and your love: "You're wonderful." "I knew you could do it." "That's incredible." "I admire what you did." "An outstanding performance." "What you did lights up my life." "I'm proud of you." "Well done!" "What a smart idea."

♥ 221 ENCOURAGING WORDS

*W*hen the way is a little bumpy, encourage a child with these lines that show you care: "Hey, you're catching on." "It's your choice." "I respect what you're doing." "You've got the winning solution." "You're really using your imagination." "You're growing up." "Keep trying, you'll get it." "You're on the right track." "I trust you."

♥ 222 ONE-WORD WONDERS

*Y*ou don't have to give a speech to show you care. Sometimes a single word will do. Try these: "Hooray," "Wow," "Great," "Bingo," "Terrific," "Magnificent," "Superb," "Excellent," "Remarkable," "Fantastic," "Incredible," "Dynamite," "Beautiful," "Exceptional," "Marvelous," "Astonishing," "Super," "Outstanding," "Perfect," "Wonderful," "Spectacular," "Phenomenal," "Remarkable," "Amazing." (Keep this list handy so you can use these expressive words.)

♥ 223 HATEFUL WORDS

*W*ith kid-help, make a list of fighting words and post it on the family bulletin board. These are words that start fights or are hurtful. Each family's list will be different but here are some common ones: "I hate you." "You stink." "I never want to play with you again." "You're a baby." See if the family can get through a day without using these words. Then try for two days, and so forth. Soon the words may not be used at all.

♥ 224 WORDS PARENTS DON'T LIKE TO HEAR

*W*hile not as bad as hateful words, these lines show a breakdown in family communication. Parents should tell children that when they feel like using these phrases, they should instead talk over the problem with parents who will lovingly listen. The phrases include: "How come I never get to . . . ?" "I could never learn that." "You never understand." "I don't know why you make me do everything." "It's not my turn." "Not now, I'll do it later." "I hate beets and all that other stuff you put on my plate." "But everyone else is doing it."

♥ 225 WORDS KIDS DON'T LIKE TO HEAR

*T*here's no love in these lines, so rule them out of *your* vocabulary: "You never do anything right." "Who do you think you are?" "I'm too busy!" "How stupid." "I never change my mind." "You think you're so smart, don't you!" "How many times do I have to tell you . . ." "Just see if I ever let you borrow it again." "Why? Because I said so."

♥ **226** WORDS PARENTS LOVE TO HEAR

*P*arents can feel they are doing a good job and teaching kids to care if they hear these lines: "What can I do to help?" "Thank you." "You're right." "How nice you look." "I'll sure think about it." "I understand what you're saying." "I'm willing to try." "I know that you love me." "This isn't as hard as I thought it would be." "Thanks for your help."

♥ **227** WORDS KIDS LOVE TO HEAR

*W*hile a parent can't say *yes* to everything, these lines show that you care: "That's okay, you tried." "We give you our permission." "I'm glad I'm your father." "I couldn't wait to hear your voice." "Let's fix it together." "I miss you." "What do *you* want to do?" "You can stay out thirty minutes later tonight."

♥ **228** THE SECRET WHISTLE

*W*hen separated in public places, it's helpful to be able to get the attention of family members. A distinctive family whistle can be the answer. In fact, it was the way a family found their eight-year-old son when he got lost in a department store in a foreign country. Practice the whistle around the house and yard so that you can be confident about using it in public. It gives everyone a secure feeling of family love and safety.

♥ 229 ON THEIR LEVEL

*Y*oung children need to be listened to. They are eager that you pay attention to the important things they want to say. To them, your listening is a sign of love. When a small child wants to talk to you, get on her level. Don't always remain in the standing I-am-taller-and-more-important-than-you position. Sit on the floor when a child is sitting on a chair. Lie down and look up at a standing child. At the least, squat down and be at her eye level. It's worth the effort to see that eager face.

♥ 230 WHEN A CHILD DIES

*B*e honest as to what has happened. Don't tell a child that his sibling or friend has just "gone away." Use the regular and normal words and patiently answer his questions. Don't hesitate to say that the love we felt for him will never go away. Discuss the impending funeral or memorial service and let the child decide whether he wants to attend. Depending on your own beliefs, talk about eternal life and the fact that this child continues to live and have interesting experiences. In daily conversation, talk about things they did together. Find out whether the school would permit the planting of a tree in the child's memory, or the gift of a special book for the library. A helpful book is *Last Week My Brother Anthony Died* (Martha Hickman, Abingdon Press, 1984), which is at most libraries.

♥ 231 KIDDIE RIDES

*M*aybe you don't have a rocking horse at your house. No matter. Be a horse yourself (on hands and knees) with child astride. Then hold him in the fireman's carry (across the shoulders). Next, try being a lifeguard and lie on the floor with your hand under your child's chin and help him "swim to shore." Let your child ride piggyback. Pretend he is a tiny baby and put him over your shoulder for a burp. These are all fun, loving ways to get in touch.

♥ 232 LOVE THAT CAKE

*S*ometimes youngsters just like to kick back and do something goofy. It helps if they know there's a goofy streak in parents, too. Make or buy a small cake. Pretend you don't have any knives to cut the cake or forks to eat with. This is a "love cake," and love cakes are hands-on. Put it in the center of the kitchen table and all of you dig in. Yes, eat the cake with your hands! It tastes sooooo good that way.

♥ 233 POETRY BABIES

*T*here's something about rhyme that soothes babies. Whether it's time for feeding, bathing, or going to sleep, don't forget to share some poetry. Poetry often expresses two essentials: the beauty of the

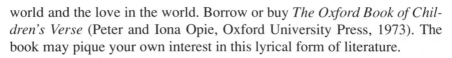

world and the love in the world. Borrow or buy *The Oxford Book of Children's Verse* (Peter and Iona Opie, Oxford University Press, 1973). The book may pique your own interest in this lyrical form of literature.

♥ 234 SAY "CHEESE" FOR SAFETY

*I*t's sad that we live in an era when children are not safe from kidnappers—including kidnapping by disgruntled spouses. One way of finding lost children is to have a really good photo. Too many parents don't take pictures regularly—and a child's appearance does change. Without alarming a child, take a good closeup photo—or have an inexpensive one taken—at least every six months. One can be the annual school photo, if it is a good full-face likeness.

♥ 235 ENVELOPES AND MORE ENVELOPES

*W*hen you'll be away for several days, write a short message to the kids for each day. Put in reminders about things to do like Scouts, tasks, TV shows, Sunday school, a party, and a special note reminding them of your love and how happy you'll be to see them soon. Date envelopes for the days you'll be away, seal the envelopes, and put them on the kitchen table so they'll be opened each morning.

♥ 236 "HOLD ME TIGHT!"

*S*ome toddlers become easily frustrated with their inability to do certain things. Then anger sets in, and sometimes a tantrum. Before it reaches that stage, pick up your child and hold him tenderly, perhaps singing to him, until the negative feelings drain away. Hold your child often—even when he isn't angry—and you'll find he's more affectionate.

♥ 237 ONE LESSON AT A TIME

*D*on't overload the system. Your love for your youngster may make you try to teach many different things at one time. A conversation should have just *one topic*: better grades, a quiet place to do homework, not using alcohol or drugs, good nutrition, parties with or without chaperons, borrowing from others, and so forth. Don't preach. Ask for ideas. At the end of the chat, summarize the one point you've made.

♥ 238 "BECAUSE *YOU* LOVE IT, I WILL TOO."

*O*ften a child's special interest is so divergent from ours that we don't bother to learn about it. Still, when a child really loves something, we ought to love it, too. A distinctive specific interest can save her from boredom and keep her out of trouble. So ask questions and get smart about your youngster's specialty, whether it is auto transmissions, surfing, painting, rocketry, modern music, or a particular author.

♥ 239 WELCOME HOME

*T*alk about a welcome home tradition—one that will let parents and kids show how happy they are to be together again as a loving family. One family gives high fives. Another gives top-of-the-head kisses. Another hugs and growls like bears and lions. It will be fun to choose your own special family tradition.

♥ 240 A TRUE LOVE STORY

♥ *WHAT'S THE SCORE?* ♥

*S*ince they already had a daughter, my folks—especially Dad—were hoping for a boy when I was born. But I chose April Fool's Day to make my entrance, and father graciously accepted a second daughter (hoping that girls, too, could appreciate the fine art of baseball). And so my baseball education began during my childhood naptimes when the radio on my bedside table was tuned to the Chicago Cubs games.

However, for my fifth birthday, there was a showdown. My mother gave me white figure skates, my father chose a baseball mitt. I accepted both gifts but much preferred the mitt, which I proceeded to break in according to tradition—rubbing it with lard every day before playing catch with two neighbor boys who put up with me because I had the only glove. I slept with the mitt between the mattress and springs of my bed "in order to teach it who's boss" according to my father's instructions. Since the Cubs played only day games then, I was always ready at dinner to answer the question, "What was the score?"

When we'd go off to Wrigley Field to watch the Cubs play, my mother would send along with us an elaborate lunch for eating in the box seats—the socially correct place for a young lady. She never knew that Dad and I ate that lunch in the car, bought seats in the bleachers, and stuffed ourselves with hot dogs. According to my father, the real fans sat in the bleachers (I noticed they bet on nearly every pitch and drank a lot of beer), and we always arrived early enough to get in the front row, where I could reach over and touch the ivy-covered brick walls of the outfield. I was admonished to watch the umpire's arms so I'd know a ball from a strike, and to keep my mitt ready should big Billy Nicholson hit a home run. Even before I'd memorized the multiplication tables, I'd memorized the lineup and kept up with the constantly changing batting averages.

My father was a raconteur and could tell baseball stories that held his audiences breathless. One time, I unexpectedly brought the high school debate team home to celebrate winning a competition. My mother, of good Swedish stock, performed a miracle of laying out a smorgasbord of meat balls, rice pudding, limpa bread, cheeses, and tarts, but it was my father who somehow fascinated the group with a detailed history of baseball bats.

Even when I went off to college, he'd inquire during our weekly phone call, "What was the score?" just to be sure I wasn't getting too engrossed in academics. And when my laundry case came back to me twice monthly, there were always clippings from the Chicago *Tribune* to keep me up-to-date on the standings.

Dad even forgave me when I married and moved far from the Cubs. I'll never forget a visit when he brought gifts for the children, including a baseball mitt for our older son. This boy dutifully listened to instructions for its use, but the minute the grandparents were back on the plane for home, he gave the mitt to his younger brother—possibly his one act of sibling kindness during their young years!

Recently when I was in Chicago, that younger son and his wife took me to a game at Wrigley Field. And yes, we sat in the bleachers. The vines were still there and the beer drinkers exceeded all expectations, but the real fans had been replaced with a chatty social group who did not watch the umpire's arms or know the lineup. Still I loved it, although I seemed to be the only one who knew the score.

At the end of his life, my ill father drifted in and out of consciousness.

One time he grasped my hand, thinking I was my mother, and thanked me for "fifty wonderful years." But another time, he very clearly asked me, "What was the score?" I told him and he smiled.

So it was through baseball that my father taught me math, loyalty, joy, and good sportsmanship, and most of all, showed me his great affection.

Now I'm searching the next generation to see who is willing to sleep with a baseball mitt under the mattress and answer that question: "What was the score?"

♥ 241 THREE-GENERATION LOVE

*J*ust as important as Mother's Day and Father's Day is the day honoring grandparents. (It's usually in September on the Sunday after Labor Day.) Telephone calls, cards, useful gifts, and celebrations are in order. Let your youngsters decide just what they want to do. If grandparents live nearby, grandchildren can make a book of coupons for services they are willing to perform: cutting the lawn, shoveling snow, gift-wrapping, running errands. For faraway grandparents, they can make an audiotape or videotape, telling about their activities and what they'd like to do when next together.

♥ 242 WHO'S IN MY BED?

*W*hen children are fussy or afraid, parents often take them into their bed. This is fine on rare occasions, but many parents make the mistake of letting babies and toddlers frequently sleep in the parents' bed. Every year there are babies suffocated by their parents, so don't do this dangerous thing! Help your young child to love his own bed and enjoy being in it. This teaches independence and is the beginning of enjoying his own space. Besides, you need your privacy and rest.

♥ 243 SCOUTS AND STREETS

*E*xplain the tradition of scouts helping older folks across streets. When out with your young child, let him pretend to be a scout, taking your arm and safely guiding you across a street or through a parking lot. Be sure to thank him for caring for you.

♥ 244 DON'T FEAR DISCIPLINE

*B*eing a parent is not a popularity contest, so don't be afraid to guide your child. If you truly love her, you will want what is in her best interest. Help her to know the difference between right and wrong, honesty and cheating, sexuality and sex, love and infatuation, peace and violence, democracy and pushiness, caring and apathy.

♥ **245** NO SEXIST STANDARDS

*W*hen making rules for youngsters, see that one sex doesn't get different standards from the other. Be sure you don't teach or imply that girls should remain sexually pure but that it's O.K. for boys to play around. Or that girls get a bigger clothing budget than guys. Or that boys are taught computer science and girls are taught homemaking. Treat your youngsters with loving equality.

♥ **246** QUILTED HANDS

*U*sing a plain quilt as a base, create a quilt for each youngster. Trace the hands of family members, then cut them out of various fabrics. Sew them in a circle, one hand just touching another, and sew them to the quilt. Embroider the child's name in the middle. An heirloom and a loving gift!

♥ **247** LOVE VERSUS HATE

*A*t supper or another time suitable for talk, bring up the subject of love versus hate. Ask children if they know synonyms for love (devotion, adoration, esteem, caring, admiration) and hate (abhorrence, malice, loathing, enmity, malignity). While this isn't a vocabulary test, a discussion of these words can follow, along with talk on how we can show love rather than hate.

116

♥ 248 LONG-DISTANCE NEATNESS

*W*hen a grandma realized her grandchildren were excessively messy, she got permission from her daughter to set up a special project with a reward. She gave the kids a list of the five things she expected: no clothes on the floor, no dishes or old food in the room, toys picked up, trash in the wastebasket, bathroom left orderly. Each week, she calls the youngsters to ask specifically how they are doing in these five areas, reminding them to be truthful! While it's a challenge, they are making progress and working toward the reward. She's says she loves them too much to let them be slobs!

♥ 249 LET'S WRITE A BOOK

*W*hen a child is bored, or when it's a rainy day, write a book with your child. Make it a simple true story, a fantasy, or a mystery. Put just a few lines on each page. Using old magazines, illustrate the story with pictures. Make a cardboard cover with the title and the young author's name. Put it where others will see it (in the family room, on the living room coffee table). Being a "published author" will do a lot for your child's self-esteem.

♥ 250 GET A LIFE!

*T*his phrase is meaningful to parents who are spending every waking moment at their jobs and at home parenting. You will be a better, more calm and loving parent if you "get a life." This means that, as much as you love your child, you must release her to the care of others so that you can have some activities on your own. These might be community service, church, classes for your own education, sports, crafts, and just time off. Share what you've been doing when you return home.

♥ 251 FEAR OF FAILURE

*M*any children shy away from activities that seem difficult, fearing they will fail and look silly. Challenge youngsters to try new things when others aren't watching. Let a child climb the tree in the backyard, try out the new bike in the early morning before the neighbor kids are awake, give the book report first to the family. Tell him that the writer John Creasey got 753 rejection slips before he published 564 books. Babe Ruth struck out 1,330 times, but also hit 714 home runs. Teach your child this adage: Don't worry about failure. Worry about the chances you miss when you don't even try.

♥ 252 IMITATE FRED ASTAIRE AND GINGER ROGERS

*O*r any famous pair of dancers you know! Play dance music as you and your child make big jumps and leaps in time with it. Then show your youngster how to hold a partner for dancing. This practice will take away the embarrassment of the first dance class or party. Learning to move with music gives a child self-confidence, long before the first prom.

♥ 253 SIBLING *UN*RIVALRY

*A*re you asked to settle arguments, take sides, soothe the wounded? You wonder why can't they love each other as much as you love them. One way to reduce sibling rivalry is to quickly separate the two fighters into separate rooms, without making any judgment. Do it the minute you hear the noise of an argument. They'll soon figure out that playing in harmony beats being alone.

♥ 254 THE BOOMING BIG BELL

*G*o to garage sales and look in catalogs for the biggest bell you can find. (Often farm catalogs have huge inexpensive bells that you can mount on a post in front of your house, but when choosing your big bell, consider the closeness of the neighbors.) When someone does something special, gather for bell ringing. Occasions might be: a very good grade on a school paper, taking off the bike training wheels, eating vegetables without arguing, the start of summer vacation, birthdays, pay raises—you decide when a little loving but noisy appreciation is needed.

♥ 255 DROP EVERYTHING

*W*ords can be as hurtful as bumps and bruises. When a child has been hurt by a playmate, immediate loving comfort from a parent is most important. Start by listening. Don't give advice or correction until the child has said everything she has to say. Then ask her what might be a solution to the problem. Only then give your own ideas in a nonjudgmental way. Tell her that it's all right to sometimes stay and argue it out with the friend, or sometimes just separate herself, joining others or coming home for comfort.

♥ 256 POSTING AN AD

*W*hen you have some tasks that need doing, write a small ad and post it on the bulletin board or the refrigerator door. Something like this: "Mom would love a helper to weed the lawn for an hourly fee." Or "Dad will provide good company for a helper who'll sort laundry." When you get a helper, make the work fun. But most important, seeking help from youngsters lets them show *their* thoughtfulness and responsibility.

♥ 257 COLLECTING

*I*t's fun and educational when family members have collections. They don't need to be expensive, so the collector can switch to something else whenever he wishes. Parents and grandparents can add to a child's collection at birthdays or when they're traveling. A collection provides a topic for child/parent discussion, and something interesting for him to display in his room, or to share at school. Consider rocks, stamps, bugs, shells, coins, postcards, marble eggs, dolls from around the world, matchbox cars, bells, pressed flowers, recipes, or carved animals. When a child gets bored with a collection, talk about handing it on to a sibling or friend. Giving and sharing are loving lessons you can teach.

♥ 258 COURT IS IN SESSION

*A*s children get older, they often get more contentious. Tell each of the arguers to write down the complaint. Then hold court and listen to both sides. This may be boring and time consuming for youngsters, but you can often determine the real reasons for the argument and settle it. Remember not to make it too easy for kids to force you to settle problems that they should learn to settle on their own.

♥ 259 GIFTS OF LOVE

*Y*ou don't want to be constantly giving gifts to your youngsters, yet it is helpful to have on hand a little supply of inexpensive gifts that you can give when the circumstances seem to call for it. These could be a magazine, a small picture frame, a ball, a bike horn, bath bubbles, a coloring book, a puzzle, stickers, a notebook, a package of morning-glory seeds, a coin purse, a little ring, a special mug.

♥ 260 COMMUTER LOVE

*W*hen you're being the chauffeur, and especially when there is just one of your children in the car, use the time for confidential talk. Don't waste these moments by driving in silence or just listening to the radio. Instead, talk about hopes and dreams and certainly how much you love your child. Don't make these one-on-one times into occasions for accusations, corrections, or interrogations. Rather let them be times of casual, loving conversations.

♥ 261 THE FACE I LOVE TO LOOK AT

*S*napshots are wonderful ways to share family times, but every now and then take a close-up of each family member. These are useful to parents for the desk at the office, in the wallet, or on the refrigerator.

Kids can send them to grandparents or exchange them with friends. They also like one of Mom and Pops for their night table.

♥ 262 TEEN TRAVELS

*P*art of launching a youngster is letting her travel without chaperons—a scary thought for some parents. Often the summer vacation between junior and senior years of high school is a good time for a trip. Four young people of the same sex can travel together. There should be some rules laid down about driving, drinking, safe accommodations, remaining together, strangers, money, and so forth. Some teens will be old enough to drive, others may travel by bus or train. Parents should have an itinerary and a nightly phone call so you always know where the travelers are. It's a good idea (and money-saving) for them to stay with relatives and friends along the way. This is a time to let go of your child, and if you've done your parenting effectively, and made the travel rules very clear, it can be a happy time for all.

♥ 263 HOME AT LAST

*W*hen you come in the door from work, you may want to just change clothes and kick back, read the mail, read the paper, and relax before making dinner. But, it's important to spend the first five minutes debriefing your child. A youngster has been away from you for a long time and has *so* many things to share. Sit on the sofa, take the child into your arms and listen for a few minutes, then go and do all those "home-again" things.

♥ 264 SUPPER FUN

*D*on't let supper be ruined by TV-watching. Enjoy your family around the table, sharing stories of the day, plans for the future, reading aloud a few pages from a good book. Comment on good happenings with lines like, "I'm pleased you did that," "That was great," "I love the way you handled the problem," or simply "I love you."

♥ 265 AFTER-SUPPER FUN

*I*t's important to be a loving family every day of the week, not just on weekends. So, after-supper activities are important in binding the family together in that space between the weekends. Sure, there's homework and the newspaper, and television shows, but they can all be put off for thirty minutes of family togetherness. Walk around the block, play a box game, go for a bicycle ride, work on a craft, go to the library, walk to the ice cream store, read a book together, make cookies, spend a few minutes learning to roller-blade or investigate some other activity that the kids enjoy.

♥ 266 THE SECRET FRIEND

*E*xplain to the family the importance of doing nice things and not taking credit for them. Parents who start this loving tradition soon find that kids follow. Secret friend deeds can include putting a supportive note or cartoon in a lunch bag, making someone else's bed, putting a flower on the table, taking out the trash without being asked, and tucking a granola bar into a briefcase. You may want to exchange names and see who can do a good deed for the other person without being found out.

♥ 267 KEEP IN TOUCH

*E*ncourage children to keep in touch with grandparents, cousins, friends who have moved away. When calling times are least expensive, let youngsters make a phone call. Help young children to choose something special to share before dialing. These calls mean much to the recipients, but are also ways to teach your child to care about others. In return, when they grow up and have their own families, they'll have the tradition of keeping in touch—with you!

♥ 268 COMPANIONSHIP AT HOME

A child's feeling that no one loves her and that she is all alone is a sadness that a parent can alleviate. While a parent is not a replacement for friends, the parent can be companionable until the child's loneliness is relieved by peers. Activities that help soothe loneliness include doing a craft or reading together on a regular basis, making a surprise for another member of the family, or planning an excursion on which a child can take a neighborhood or school acquaintance. Reassure her of her importance in the family and how much you love her at this very moment.

♥ 269 THE LOVE MAP

*P*ut a large map on the wall of the kitchen or family room (a U.S. or world map is best). With a star or thumbtack, note the places that relatives and good friends live. Then with a highlighter pen, trace the routes of your family trips. When the time comes to decide on your next vacation, the map will help. Be sure to ask youngsters for trip ideas, rather than just announcing where you'll all be going.

♥ 270 TEACHER SAYS

*M*any teachers say that lack of goals is one of the chief reasons for poor school performance. So many youngsters have ability but just don't use it, and even if they set goals, they are too low. As a parent, show your youngster the joys of facing challenges. Say, "Because I love you so much I don't want you to have a boring life." See that your children experience museums, plays, new sports and lessons, rather than just having dull, routine days. Remember the saying: Aim low—boring. Aim high—soaring.

♥ 271 NO CRABBY WITCH, NO OLD NAG

*T*each a child that it is respectful and loving to listen and obey the *first* time you ask him to do something. That way you won't become a crabby witch or an old nag.

♥ 272 LITERARY AND TV/MOVIE LOVE

*W*hen reading with children, note how the story characters express love and caring. Note what words the characters use to put these feelings into words. Point out some examples; let kids find others. Also comment on characters that aren't kind and loving. When a child sees a loving scene on the TV or movie screen, talk about it later. What words were used? Was it a nice kind of love that showed how people were considerate of each other? How else did characters show they cared? Did love make a difference in the outcome of the story?

♥ 273 DRIVER'S ED—HOME STYLE

*W*hile your youngster will probably take a driver's education course in high school, your own driving class can begin years earlier. This is a way to show that you care for their safety. First, remember that kids are copycats, so your driving example is very important. Let a child monitor your speedometer so you don't break the law. Check if it is okay to turn or change lanes and let a child double-check. Let your youngster read the road signs to you. Show and explain all the gauges and buttons on the dashboard. In your own driveway, let a child practice steering the car. Start a fund for the youngster's first car and agree to match her earnings so that a safe older car can be bought when she has a license and has demonstrated responsibility.

♥ 274 "MY GREAT AND GOOD LIST"

A child may behave as if he feels worthless—don't let that kind of thinking get a foothold. To build self-esteem and the knowledge that he is loved, help him create a list of one or more really good things he has done in the past. Put the list where the youngster can see it (the drawer of his bed table is a good place). Make an effort to find good things to add to the list, no matter how small. Encourage him to add to the list, too. Look at it each night at bedtime and compliment him on this growing list of great and good things. This is just between parent and child and not for sharing with the other kids.

♥ 275 WHAT MOTHER TAUGHT ME

*V*ery often a mother (or father) passes on to a child the loving words of wisdom from her own mother. One little rhyme from a mother to a daughter falls in this category. Help your child memorize it.

> Don't look for the flaws in life,
> But even if you find them,
> Be wise and kind, and somewhat blind,
> And look for the virtues behind them.

♥ ♥ ♥ ♥ ♥ ♥ ♥ ♥ ♥ ♥ ♥ ♥ ♥ ♥ ♥ *365 WAYS!*

♥ **276** THE BENEFITS OF HUGS

*F*or some, the words *I love you* are hard to say. A kiss can be too mushy for some kids. But a hug is just right. Show your youngster love through hugs, and teach him to hug in return. A good saying is: A hug is a great gift; one size fits all and it's easy to exchange.

♥ **277** WHAT *WE* KNOW

*R*espect your youngster's intelligence by not talking down to her and trying never to talk over her head, either. Children appreciate that feeling of being equal with a parent. Use the phrase "what you and I know." Develop a special area of expertise with each child. Talk about computers and soccer with your daughter, music and museums with your son, always expanding "what we know."

♥ **278** SILLY SARDINES

*T*his is a fun and fast after-dinner game. One person hides. Moving very quietly, others look for him. When someone finds him, they put their arms around each other and hide close together like sardines. When a third person finds the first two, they join in a giant hug, hide together, and so on. The first one to find the hider is the next one to hide.

♥ 279 "HOW ARE YOU?"

*F*ine or *Okay* are the usual, thoughtless answers. But, as a loving parent, you want to inquire about how a child feels without turning him into a hypochondriac. Don't indicate that you think a child is sick when it is really something else bothering him. Help him overcome moody or sluggish feelings through understanding and love. Get the facts, then show you care. Don't let him dwell on negative feelings, but rather talk about and encourage well-being, energy, a happy attitude.

♥ 280 REALLY REACHING

*A*s an extension of your family's love, reach out to others who need help. Talk together as a family about a service project—not just at the holidays, but during the year. Contact your local social services agency and find a project your family will enjoy. It may mean distributing clothes, serving meals at a shelter, delivering meals to the homebound, collecting blankets, or giving a program or party at a care facility. Show that your love doesn't ever run out.

♥ 281 CERTIFICATES OF LOVE

*M*ake a little booklet of handmade certificates that your youngster can redeem from you. The certificates can purchase a trip to the zoo, a day without chores, his favorite meal, a video party with friends, a manicure and pedicure, free admission to an event, an oil change and car wash for a teen's car, a new audiocassette, a three dollar "discount" at the toy store, an up-front seat in the car for one week.

♥ 282 WORKING KIDS

*I*t's important for young people to understand why their parents work and just what they do. Many companies, and even cities, have special days when parents are encouraged to bring kids to the workplace. Let them sit alongside you and participate when appropriate: suggesting ideas and even solutions to problems, keying in material on the computer, sealing mail, sharpening pencils, delivering memos, sorting incoming mail, listing and prioritizing your tasks, placing phone calls for you. You don't want the business world to be a mystery place, so let your youngster share and understand your business day and why you're often tired at night. It can be fun and beneficial to both of you.

♥ 283 ROOM SERVICE

*S*urprise a child when she's getting ready for bed by bringing a snack tray (milk and a cracker is enough) to her room. Sit down and chat about the day. She'll feel very loved to have you waiting on her with this treat.

♥ 284 THE LOVE OF LEARNING

*P*roviding a good education at home and supporting education at school is a sure sign of your love. Sometimes this will be difficult when a child has trouble learning, but hang in there. Tell him that you love him too much to let him be uneducated. Remember the saying: If you think education is expensive, try ignorance.

♥ 285 NONJUDGMENTAL SHOPPING FOR CLOTHES

*K*ids' clothes can be expensive—and they often grow out of them quickly—so getting your money's worth is important. Shop together with your preteen so she can explain to you the importance (to herself and her friends) of current fashions. But ahead of time, make some parameters about what is and isn't acceptable to you. Discourage the wearing of gang clothing by talking with other parents and agreeing not to buy it. Fashionable clothes need not be expensive if you wait for sales or shop at discount stores or factory outlets. In fact, by the time a youngster is twelve years old, put her on a clothing budget. That way, she can have some choices on how to spend the money. If she buys an expensive trendy rhinestone-studded blouse and a month later it's out of style at her school, she will have learned a valuable lesson. Because you love your child you want her to look good (or at least not too outlandish), but you also want her to be comfortable and happy about the way she looks.

♥ 286 NONJUDGMENTAL HAIR AND MAKEUP STYLES

*W*hen children are young, talk about hair styles and also what makeup can do. When out together, be good observers. Spend money on a makeup session for a daughter, but don't be pressured to buy more products than she really needs. Over the upcoming years, this makeup session will save you a lot of money that might be spent for cosmetics that are experimented with once and then left idle in the drawer. Set a budget for makeup purchases so she will be careful about what she buys. Permit hair fads as long as the hair is not being damaged and the hair is always clean. You may be upset or startled by some teen fads, but remember that fashions don't last long. Because you love your youngster, just be glad that hair styles are not nearly as important as living a life free from alcohol and drugs.

♥ 287 REUNION TIME

*F*amily reunions are great occasions for sharing love. Plan well ahead (at least six months) so that almost everyone can come. Let each family bring a favorite dish for the first potluck supper. Plan sports, relays, and activities for all ages. Share photo albums and take lots of pictures of the events, including one group photo. Have a storytelling night for listening to tales by young and old. At the last meal, have an emcee give awards for those who came the farthest and the shortest distances, for the oldest and youngest, for the funniest story or joke, and so forth.

♥ 288 NO SNOOPING

A youngster's room is his private domain. Parents who have loving trust in their children do not snoop in the room. (The only exceptions are if you suspect that drugs or stolen property—jewelry, leather goods, street signs, or electronic equipment—may be stashed in the room, or you believe that illegal activities are taking place there.) Let a child arrange the room and the wall decor as he pleases. The once-a-week cleanup (to foil the rodents) is your only request.

♥ 289 BEST-FRIEND DAY

*T*his unofficial holiday can be celebrated anytime you want to honor friendship. It's important to teach kids how to be appreciative and loving. A week or so in advance of this "holiday," let each family member invite a best friend to the event. Parents and children should plan a few simple activities of interest to both generations: supper in front of the fireplace, an after-supper walk or game, a special video.

♥ 290 QUIET CONVERSATION

*I*f you find it uncomfortable to just sit down and have a serious talk with your teen, try to combine conversation with some other activity. Sometimes your loving concern will come through better when the lights aren't too bright. Try these occasions for talk: in the car at night, in the hot tub, outside looking up at the stars. One mother says she gets a lot of conversation from her daughter while she's giving her a back rub!

♥ 291 WARM FUZZIES

*T*his is the popular name for notes of love and encouragement from parent to child. Warm fuzzies can be as long as a sonnet or letter, or as short as the phrases "I love you, Laurie," or "Dear Lisa, things will be better tomorrow," or "Steve, you're the greatest!" Leave the warm fuzzie in a drawer, on a mirror, in a pocket or purse, or under the bed pillow. You'll find that children will treasure these private loving messages.

♥ 292 WHAT'S MANLY?

*T*here's a big difference between manly and macho. The entire family needs to talk about this—not just fathers with sons. A man can be caring, appreciative, and loving without being wimpish. Good manners, a well-modulated voice and good vocabulary, and consideration of others regardless of sex should be encouraged instead of a show-off, big-timer attitude, and offensive language.

♥ 293 THE GRANDPARENT CONNECTION

*S*ometimes the opportunities to develop a personal loving relationship between grandparents and their grandchildren is limited to holiday celebrations. Unlike ages past when grandparents were part of the resident family, a youngster today often doesn't relate to, appreciate, or really know the grandparents and vice versa. One grandfather says he's solved that problem this way: When one of his grandchildren reaches the age of sixteen, he or she is invited to spend an entire week at his home. He says that he and his wife probably spoil the kid with affection and attention, but he believes such special privileges are mutually beneficial. Activities are chosen to meet the teen's interests: theater, fishing, music, trips to museums and botanical gardens, and so forth. The time spent together stimulates family continuity, family pride, family love.

♥ 294 SHARING THE NEWS

*T*he daily newspaper can be a big boost for parent/child relationships. Loving parents care that their children are aware of what's going on in the world. It is bonding and educational for a parent and child to sit together and read the paper. Each can point out articles of interest. Big words and concepts can be explained. Fears can be allayed. A good article can be shared with the entire family at the dinner table.

♥ 295 CRYING BABY

*S*tart when children are young to encourage expressions of love and caring. When a baby is crying, ask an older child to comfort the baby, hug her, and entertain her. Say, for example, "Scotty, will you please give the baby some love?" As children grow, continue this idea of giving loving support to a sibling. Be especially appreciative when this happens. Learning to be a caring person is a great lesson and it starts with a parent's example of compassion.

♥ 296 PET'S DAY

*C*hoose a day to honor all the pets in the family—or even in the neighborhood. On their official birthday each year, let dogs and cats wear bows. Put balloons on fishbowls and birdcages. Plan a yard picnic with the pets as guests. Talk about when you got them, what tricks they've learned, and how much love they have brought into the family.

♥ 297 LAP-SITTING

*T*here is the saying "You may outgrow your parents' laps, but you'll never outgrow their hearts." Lap-sitting is usually associated with young children, but it doesn't have to be. When your youngster gets too big to sit on your lap, try sitting on his!

♥ 298 SEPARATE BUT EQUAL

*W*hen there are several children in the family, sometimes one or two appear to be good and the other difficult. One child may bring home many stars or awards from school. Another may be a winning soccer player and have lots of friends. Another may not yet have found any area of excellence. But a parent has to love each child equally, although it may be shown in different ways. It's very important for a child, especially one who doesn't get much public acclaim, to be told that you love him, and also be told this in front of other family members. You will always love your children, but you will love them for different reasons. It may be easier to love the good and achieving child, but you can say to a challenging child: "I love you because you make me stretch as a parent." "You're a great guy—don't hide it."

♥ 299 JUST BECAUSE

*I*t doesn't have to be a holiday to give a little gift. On no occasion at all, slip a small gift under a child's pillow. It needn't be expensive; sometimes it's just a giveaway that comes in the mail. Parents may find that they get "just because" items under their pillows, too.

♥ 300 A TRUE LOVE STORY

♥ *LEARNING LOVE IN REVERSE* ♥

*B*abies are supposed to be cuddled and loved—Chad's mother knew that. But it wasn't easy, since demonstrations of love had never been an element in the history of her third-generation dysfunctional family. One's own self came first, and babies were just another demand on an already demanding life. But Chad didn't know that. Even when she and her husband were shouting at each other, Chad would try to intervene with baby kisses.

Both parents were writers, each rather self-centered, and so wrapped up in their work that they didn't have the time or ability to show affection to their son. Then came the divorce. Still, Chad thrived. The first day of kindergarten, he put his arms around a crying girl and asked, "What's the matter?" On his first visit to the big city of San Francisco, he kissed the dusty windows of the cable car to show his joy. Even when he was to get an inoculation, he fearlessly leaped into the doctor's lap and held out his arm.

Amazed as his mother was, she didn't know how to respond to Chad's unconditional love because she had no example of family affection. A glimmer of understanding came when they rented rooms in a house filled with a large family. Chad loved the interaction of this caring, noisy group, and his mother was grateful for their encouragement of her plan to go to a community college to prepare for a new career.

When Chad was almost seven, they moved again, but this time to a distant state. Everything here was different, except Chad, who loved his mother through the stresses of two years of graduate school, two years of temporary jobs, and finally a new position in her chosen field. But now her time was taken up with getting ahead, making money, finding better housing, and investigating the best schools and summer camps. She figured that if she couldn't verbalize her love for him, she would provide for his every need.

It was then that she started to truly listen to the church services she attended while Chad was in Sunday school. He had eagerly told her that the Bible says "God is Love" and that Jesus taught us to love one another. As the months went by, this more spiritual kind of love that she began to feel soon developed into sensitivity to the feelings of others, awareness of the beauty of their surroundings, and an appreciation of Chad's growing independence.

She was surprised that when Chad left for college, her own growing sense of love for others filled what she thought would be a tremendous void. She realized he was not abandoning her, but rather asserting his independence. Each time he fell in and out of love during his college years, she was able to understand and commiserate, for she too had some heartbreaking relationships. But those no longer sent her into despair, for she had found that real love has no end. When her tall, manly, protective son returned home, he had matured beyond his role as a loving son; he was now a good friend—and someone she greatly loved.

Having at last found the ability to express love to her son, she was able to easily share him as he left for a successful career in communications and a marriage to a loving and outgoing woman. In looking back, Chad finds no fault, for he says that his upbringing consisted of opportunities to be caring of others.

While most parents give from the heart—as well as the pocketbook— to love a child, and thus enjoy a family where love flows freely from parent to child, for Chad's mother it was the other way around. Having a naturally affectionate son eventually showed her that love begins right in our own thoughts and words and actions.

♥ 301 SING-ALONG LOVE

*W*hen taking a long car trip, spend some time singing together, but once in a while, give your songs a love theme. The word *love* has to be somewhere in the song. Consider "Love Makes the World Go 'Round," "I Love You, You Love Me," "This Can't Be Love," "The Look of Love," "Love Is a Many-splendored Thing," "Our Love Is Here to Stay," or "Jesus Loves Me" for starters. It doesn't matter if some don't know a song, they may learn it by humming along.

♥ 302 HAPPY HANUKKAH

*T*his Jewish holiday is also called the Feast of Lights or Feast of Dedication. It usually occurs in December and lasts eight days. It has an interesting history that you may want to read from the encyclopedia or books such as *The Hanukkah Book* (Marilyn Burns, Scholastic Press, 1981). Candles are lighted each day, charitable contributions are made, and gifts are exchanged. If this holiday is not one your family celebrates, it is important that you discuss it with your children. Set an example of love and appreciation for all humankind—all religions and races—and instill this loving respect in your children.

♥ 303 IF YOU LOVED ME, YOU'D SAY *YES*

*S*ometimes our love sends up a red flag and tells us we can't give in to a child's request. But often we can modify our answer so that it does include a *yes*. This makes it easier for a child to accept. When a child makes a request, hoping for a yes answer, and you feel inclined to say no, consider a way to say yes first.

Example 1:
Child: I'm short of cash, can you give me some money?
Parent: No, you've been foolish and will have to wait for your allowance.
Better Parent: Yes, I'll be paying allowances in just two days.
Example 2:
Child: Can you take me to Susie's house?
Parent: No way—it's raining cats and dogs.
Better Parent: Yes, as soon as this storm lets up.
Example 3:
Child: Can I have some ice cream?
Parent: No, we're having dinner in half an hour.
Better Parent: Yes, that's a good idea for our dessert.

♥ 304 PRESIDENT-FOR-THE-DAY

*L*et a child choose a special day each year when he will be totally in charge. Everyone must obey him. He will decide what is served at meals (ice cream for breakfast?), where each person sits at the table, where the family goes for an excursion and who gets the front seat in the car, what games are played and TV shows viewed, what the bedtimes are. Of course, a good president will delegate authority and assign his own chores to others, remembering to be reasonable, since a sibling will be president another day. Still, he'll feel pretty special after twenty-four hours of this!

♥ 305 WHY?

*A*s often as possible, explain to your child *why* he can't do something, rather than just saying no. For example, he can't take gum from the grocery store without paying for it because it isn't honest. Let him see that the *activity* is what is wrong so he doesn't think *he* is wrong or bad. Tell him that he is good and loved, and his intelligence will keep him from being tempted to do a bad thing.

♥ 306 "HELP THE ONE WHO'S BEHIND"

*S*o often the family is rushing to get out the door: getting dressed, feeding the dog, finishing eating, gathering things to take along—it's wild! Teach family members who need assistance to shout, "Help the one who's behind." When others call back "Who's behind?" the one in need of help shouts his name. It's fun to come to the rescue. Giving help when requested is a sign of caring.

♥ 307 SHARING SUPPER

*W*ith the family, talk about your love for one another and how some people are alone and may not have anyone to love them. Plan to share a simple supper with someone who doesn't have many friends. This could be a senior citizen in your neighborhood, a widowed relative, a new friend from church, or a foreign-exchange student. Work as a family to make the meal and clean up. Help your child find conversational topics and some activity, such as an indoor or outdoor game, to share after supper.

♥ 308 FEED THE BIRDS

*M*ake a comparison between your love for a child and a mother bird's love for her babies. (If you have a cat and kitten or dog and puppy, you can use that example as well.) Show how the mother feeds her babies, keeps them warm, protects them from danger—just as you do for your child. Care for hungry birds in the cold winter by hanging and filling an inexpensive bird feeder. Talk about caring for birds and other small animals as opposed to killing them for target practice. Be supportive of your local animal-care agencies and go to visit them just to look.

♥ 309 DEFUSING ANGER

*S*how a younger child how much you love her and want her to be happy by helping her defuse her anger. Rather than hitting, biting, or throwing things, try these alternate ways of working off the fury: throwing balls against the garage door, beating the bed with a pillow, hammering nails into an old piece of wood, tearing newspapers into little pieces. Only when the anger is gone can you sit down and talk about the cause of the anger and then find some solutions.

♥ 310 WONDERFUL WARM BATH

*W*ho says a bath has to be at bedtime? Sometimes a warm bath can be restful when tired, soothing when tense, comforting when angry. While you can only recommend this soothing time to teens, you can lovingly lead little ones to a bubbly tub bath to help them calm down while you read to them.

♥ 311 LATCHKEY MESSAGES

*F*or the child returning to an empty house, your reassurance and love is necessary. It doesn't take much time to leave a message on a tape recorder—it's probably quicker than writing a note. Your message will give some instructions about free time, homework, starting supper, keeping safe. But also include something fun, like a suggestion for a special snack or an announcement of an upcoming event. With a message on tape, the child can play it as many times as she wants or needs.

♥ 312 WHEN A PET DIES

*D*on't say the pet ran away or went to sleep (then kids might fear going to sleep). Talk about how much the family loved the pet and how much love the pet expressed. If kids want to know why the pet died, give a simple truthful explanation. Say, "Sometimes a pet gets sick and cannot stay here with us anymore. That's what happened to Chipper, but our family is going to stick together." Give a few nonmorbid details, answer questions. Be very sympathetic. Reassure a child that the death wasn't his fault. Perhaps you'll want to help the child plan a little memorial service. Read Genesis 1:20-25 and I John 2:25, or Psalm 23. Let each person share a happy story about the pet. A good book about a pet that dies is *The Tenth Good Thing About Barney* (Judith Viorst, Macmillan, 1975).

♥ 313 HEAD OF THE TABLE

A parent doesn't always have to sit at the head of the table at a meal. Let youngsters have the honor, say the grace, serve the food, lead the table discussions, decide when everyone can be excused, and clear the table. This adds to a child's poise and sense of self-worth.

♥ 314 PAINTED HEARTS

*W*atercolor paint washes off easily, so be colorful and bold when a child does something that should be greatly appreciated. Paint the glass on the front door with hearts and the child's name. Or paint a love word on the bathroom mirror. For younger children, paint the bathtub, and watch your work disappear as the water moves up the sides.

♥ 315 BUSY, BUSY

*F*or those days when you don't have time to interact with your youngster, you can still keep in touch and show that you care. When a child is doing something in one room of the house and you are busy in another room, take a one-minute break every fifteen minutes or so. Just poke your head into the room where she's working or playing and ask, "How's it going?" That way you get a quick report, and she's aware that you care even when you can't be together.

♥ 316 IT'S A GIFT?

*C*hildren sometimes have the need to *give* you something. They may wrap up a favorite toy, a dead lizard, a flower, or the last cookie. It's a love offering, and you must accept it as a gift given from the heart (even the lizard) with appreciation and love. You love the gift because you love your child!

♥ 317 A TRUE THANKSGIVING

*R*emember the pilgrims? One pilgrim mother didn't do all the cooking for that first Thanksgiving celebration; each family brought something to the feast. So today, rather than overworking one cook, make the feast a potluck affair, with the host family doing the turkey and stuffing and others bringing potatoes, vegetables, salads, and dessert. Early in November, discuss with the family the importance of reaching out to others. Think of someone who is without family at this holiday time to invite to your gathering. Show your children how to share love by helping them to be gracious young hosts and hostesses. Be sure you compliment them afterwards.

♥ 318 THANKSGIVING GRATITUDE

*O*n this official day of giving thanks, plan to do more than just feast. Of course, you can have grace before the dinner. But also use this occasion as a day to express your love and appreciation for each family member. Have a time when you can tell each child (and your spouse) how grateful you are that they are part of the family. You may want to make a little list for each one, telling some of the things he does that make you love him so very much.

♥ 319 IN HONOR OF . . .

*W*hen it is a child's birthday, consult with the school librarian and give a new book to the library. Put a bookplate in the front with wording such as "In honor of Katie Keller's eighth birthday." Maybe you can make the presentation in the classroom. This shows that you love your child enough to emphasize the importance of reading.

♥ 320 SNACK-AND-SHARE NIGHT

*S*ometimes we need to encourage youngsters to feel comfortable when they talk and confide in us. One father invented "Snack and Share Night." Using a big sheet and many pillows, he created a comfy game area in the living room, where parents and children gathered in a circle, with a board game in the middle. Supper consisted of various finger foods, and the snacks were rotated. This supper event resulted in good conversation and sharing, plus a warm feeling in the family.

♥ 321 A SECRET

*W*e all love being confided in. Tell your child a secret, something "only between you and me." It's a good way to teach children to be confidential, and your child feels special when you trust him.

♥ 322 CHRISTMAS LOVE

*S*ome kids think that their parents' love for them is shown by many Christmas gifts. But love is much more than receiving, it includes giving. Show your love to your youngsters by helping kids to share love outside the family circle at this season. "Love projects" include: adopting a needy family, helping give a party at a seniors or youth facility, asking how you can help an elderly neighbor, including a student from another country in your family celebration, caroling for neighbors and shut-ins, volunteering to serve meals at a homeless shelter, making a gingerbread house with a child whose parents both work, making extra batches of cookies to give to busy families, providing supper for a person with a disability, babysitting for busy parents so they can shop, taking part in a toy or food drive, telephoning faraway friends and relatives, and making ornaments to give to friends, teachers and neighbors. When you give love in these ways, you haven't lost anything but a little time, and you've gained much emotional satisfaction.

♥ 323 THE BEST-EVER CHRISTMAS

*D*on't make Christmas *for* children, make it *with* them. Let them know the joys of surprises, helping others, shopping, and decorating. At Christmas we celebrate God's *loving* the world enough to send Jesus to us. So love is the theme of Christmas, not gift-getting. Start traditions such as going caroling, handmaking gifts and gift papers, putting decorations in every room, including the bathroom, taking a drive to see outdoor decorations, going to a Christmas Eve church service, or adopting a needy family. For more ideas, read my book *101 Ideas for the Best-ever Christmas* (Abingdon Press, 1992).

♥ 324 LOVE MY BEDROOM!

*I*t doesn't make any difference if your child's bedroom furnishings are old or new. At bedtime, in the semidark, talk about them. Make up fantastic stories about everything. "The wallpaper was hand-painted by Goldilocks." "A king once slept in this bed." "The window frame is made of pure gold." "This blanket was made from my great-great-great aunt's hair." "This teddy bear has been to the moon." Love that bedroom!

♥ 325 BONDING BOSH

*S*ome "experts" have said that a parent must bond with a new baby immediately or both will be psychologically damaged. Of course, it is important to develop a lasting, loving tie with a baby, but illness, adoption, or other conditions may prevent it from happening at the moment of birth. The myth of early bonding has given many parents a lot of guilt. Now, new research shows that the bond can be made at any time, and in most cases it will last a lifetime. For more on this issue, read *Mother-Infant Bonding: A Scientific Fiction* (Diane E. Eyer, Yale University Press, 1993).

♥ 326 THE SECRET WORD

*S*ecrets can bind a family closer together. Talk with the family about a secret word that means *love*. Onc family uses *Sweetnick;* another has chosen *Evol,* which is *love* spelled backward; our family likes RILY, for *Remember I Love You.* Create your own special secret word and use it frequently. It's fun!

♥ 327 LIVING SCRAPBOOK

*B*uy an inexpensive scrapbook. Let a child print the name of the current month with a crayon, and then paste in items contributed by the family—a scorecard from a ball game, a good school paper, a loving letter from Grandma, a recital program, photos, a baby announcement. The child can write explanatory comments as needed. Add to the scrapbook each week, and let a different child be in charge the next month. At the end of the year, it will be a record of an active and loving family.

♥ 328 TALK ABOUT ABUSE

*O*ut of great love for your child, and with no intention of scaring him, have a serious talk about abuse. Tell your child that no one has the right to batter or molest him and that you will do everything possible to protect him. Consider acting out special situations: responding to a bully, answering the doorbell or telephone when alone, what to do when being followed, when someone tries to pick him up, when someone tries to touch him in a private place. Be calm. Be honest. Be reassuring. But most of all, see that your child has this critical knowledge.

♥ 329 TRIPLE HUG

*P*arents can scoop up a small child into a three-way hug. See if you can get all noses together! Practice giving three kisses at the same time.

♥ 330 HAPPY HOUSE

*W*ith the help of a youngster, use various-sized cardboard boxes to create a house or apartment building for small dolls to live in. Cut doors and windows. Let the child draw pictures on the walls: a fireplace, book shelves, kitchen cupboards, and so forth. Make simple furniture out of cardboard. Then create situations and, together, act out the solutions: the baby is crying, a party is being planned, dad burns his hand on the stove, junior can't find his homework, big sister is on the telephone for an hour. Let the solutions lead to a loving, happy household.

♥ 331 SHARING WORK

*O*nce in a while, work alongside your child as she does her chores. This can be a time of closeness and love. And you will be reassured that the child understands how to do the work. Don't be critical, but it's okay to point out an improvement. Once in a while, do one of her chores for her—"Just because I feel like doing something special for you."

♥ 332 PARENT-TO-PARENT LOVE

*Y*oungsters form ideas on marriage from what they observe at home. Certainly a happy marriage sets a fine example, but kids also can learn good lessons from a divorce. Don't let your own bad experience make

153

your child wary of love and marriage. Talk often about the good things that happen when two people love each other. Include these wise sayings:

Love does not consist of two people looking *at* each other, but of two people looking in the same direction.

Even when a marriage is made in heaven, the maintenance work has to be done here on earth.

Building a happy relationship is not a task, it's an opportunity.

Be flexible—remember that time is like a dressmaker specializing in alterations.

♥ 333 GOING IT ALONE?

*S*ingle parents know the importance of extra love for their kids after the divorce or death of a spouse. A big help to single parents is companionship with other families—seek them out for social activities. Plan to do something together several times a month. This gives youngsters a sense of belonging to an expanded family and can result in "brother-sister" relationships. For more ideas, read my book *Single with Children* (Abingdon Press, 1993).

♥ 334 SECRET IMPROVEMENT

*Y*our heart goes out to a child with a problem such as excessive weight, clumsiness, severe skin blemishes, and so forth. While not as serious as many physical handicaps, children do feel embarrassed and undesirable with these problems. Don't make it an issue for the entire family. Instead, work quietly and confidentially with the youngster to design a program of improvement. Don't announce what you're doing, just work diligently and give encouragement on a one-to-one basis. Others will soon see the results.

♥ 335 RUBBING NOSES

*E*skimos supposedly use this as a loving greeting. But it's also fun for young children. Find a book about Eskimos and read it when you introduce this idea.

♥ 336 RUBBING ELBOWS

*A*n ancient African tribe used this method of extending a peaceful and loving welcome. (We still use the phrase today to mean getting together with people.) Youngsters think it's fun to try to rub both elbows (that means there will be four elbows meeting).

♥ 337 WEDGES

*U*nsolved problems within the family are like wedges—they force a family apart and replace love with disaffection. Start when kids are young to solve problems rather than let them continue. Make a list of family problems that involve the children and take them up one at a time when the whole family has time to share ideas. Problem solving involves five steps: (1) gathering the facts, (2) stating the problem concisely, (3) listing possible solutions, (4) considering each alternative, and (5) making a decision for now and agreeing to try it. Insist on kindness during the discussion. The ability to solve problems can be a great gift to youngsters of all ages.

♥ **338** MY BAG

*L*ittle kids love to carry around a container with toys inside. Use an old handbag, sport bag, or attache case for this purpose. Put safe, small toys (including an unbreakable mirror) in all the compartments. With the child, look in the mirror and say, "I see the one I love!" The bag may also be big enough for that "blankie." When going to day care or grandpa's, let her take her bag along.

♥ **339** UNSOLVED MYSTERIES

*T*ry not to let a child go to bed worried about something; help him resolve the problem before he goes to sleep. Or, if no resolution is possible that evening, show you care by setting a specific time to talk about it the next day. Be casual about the problem and call it an unsolved mystery. Don't forget a hug and the line, "I know we can figure this out."

♥ 340 WHEN KIDS DON'T FOLLOW YOUR PLANS

*Y*oungsters often do the unexpected. They may decide not to go on to college, but work instead. They may drop out of your family's religion. They may adopt a life-style that's different from yours. They may marry someone you don't like. But this is *their* life, not yours. You've set the example and done your best. Now, just love them and release them.

♥ 341 THE MOOSH MONSTER ATTACKS

*I*t's good to be silly now and then—especially after a hard day at work or after a serious family episode is resolved. Turn out the lights in the house and let family members crawl around in the dark—not to scare anyone, but to see if they can plant a big mooshy kiss on someone. Let yourself be caught often to add to the fun.

♥ 342 DECISIONS, DECISIONS

*A*lthough it is faster to make all the decisions yourself, it shows love and respect to involve youngsters in as many decisions as possible. Give kids choices when it comes to selecting after-school activities, arranging their bedroom, buying a birthday gift for a party, selecting a new school outfit. This kind of parental love gives a child many choices, but it does not give him the choices he is too young to make. True parental love frees a child to be self-governing.

♥ 343 CURB YOUR LOVE

*I*n our desire to keep youngsters safe, we sometimes over-protect. A New York City mom had taught her first-grader how to carefully cross a major street on the way to school. After accompanying him the first week, she then remained at the corner during the second week. Then he was to be on his own. But the mother snuck out the third week to watch him return home. He spotted her at the corner and said, "I know you care, but do you have to care so much? I don't like it that you don't trust me." The mother realized her actions were hampering rather than helping, and she learned to curb her love, as she says "in a gradual weaning process." From then on, in other areas, she taught her son what was expected of him and then trusted him to act intelligently.

♥ 344 LEAVING WITH LOVE

A young child is often confused by grandparents and other adults who come into her life and then suddenly disappear. One set of grandparents handled it this way. Several days ahead of their departure, they talked about going to their own home, and they showed pictures of where they were going. They gave the grandchild one picture to keep and told her that she would come and visit there sometime. The night before they left (they were leaving very early in the morning), they took extra tuck-in time and after she had fallen asleep, they put a little gift on the foot of her bed. All these actions helped to make their departure easier to accept. The little girl knew that they loved her, and she eagerly awaited their next visit.

♥ 345 THE PEST

*W*hen you're busy and a child pesters you, the inclination is to send the child away. But he's usually back all too soon. You'll save your precious time and show him you care by taking just a minute to find the need. If it can't be quickly settled, set a time to talk about it. If the child is bored and seems to need your company, involve the child in the task you're doing.

♥ 346 A PLAY PEN?

*M*any parents think it is not kind and loving to put a baby or toddler in a playpen. Not so! Considering the size of the baby in proportion to the playpen, it's like playing in a small room. Most important, it teaches a young child to be independent and play alone for fifteen to thirty minutes twice or more each day. It is also the safest place your child can be as you work on a project or answer the door or phone. Put toys in the playpen that are not available elsewhere. Affix a shoebag to the side wall of the playpen and fill it with small toys. The youngster will be happily occupied in taking each one out and inspecting it. If a toddler tries to climb out, firmly put him back with the word *no*. Start to use a playpen when a baby is a few months old so he will be accustomed to it and look forward to being in it.

♥ 347 A SYMBOL OF LOVE

*R*ings have long been symbols of love. They are unending, unbroken circles, reminders that we are always loved. Take your youngsters—boys and girls—to a variety store where inexpensive rings are sold. Let each pick out one. A girl may want to wear hers on a finger, a boy will usually prefer to put his on his key chain or notebook ring. Let these be reminders of your unconditional, unbroken love.

♥ 348 MIDNIGHT MEMENTOS

*A*s you go out the door for an evening event, promise your child you'll leave a memento on the foot of her bed when you return. This can be the program from the play, the mint from the restaurant, the ticket stub from the game or movie, or a scribbled note, "Home at midnight—I love the way you look curled up asleep."

♥ 349 COMPUTER LOVE MESSAGES

*A*s youngsters become proficient in using the computer, create a document for messages, such as "Aaron: it's great you ate your entire breakfast," "Mom, remember to get cookies for the sleep-over this weekend," "Lindsay: Wow, I didn't have to remind you of anything today," "Claire: I love your hugs." The messages can be anonymous or signed, and can be left in the computer for others to find or printed out and tucked in pockets and lunch boxes, put on a mirror or window, or in a drawer or bed. As children get older, you may want to use the computer for reminders and more important messages.

♥ 350 GUNS AND KIDS

*D*on't have guns where kids can have access to them. If you need guns for protection (or if you take pleasure in killing animals), at least have your guns and ammunition locked up. A loving family certainly doesn't want to harm one of its members. Far too many children are accidently killed or injured by guns that were accessible.

♥ 351 GUNS AND ANIMALS

*C*hildren should be taught to love and respect animals and all nature, so teach them not to think it is a sport to kill birds and small animals. If population control of animals is needed, subscribe to a more humane way of thinning out range animals. If killing is not the object, but rather target practice, good aim can be practiced at organized pistol ranges, through archery, bowling, dart games, and so forth. The compassion and love we have for one another should be extended to animals as well.

♥ 352 SECRET MESSAGE

*M*any families have a secret way of writing "I love you." It may be a heart or a smiling face or a big X. Tiny notes (the little papers with adhesive on the back) can be used for your secret message and stuck on the inside band of a cap, on the toe of a pair of shoes in the closet, on a bicycle handle.

♥ 353 FIND SOMEONE YOU LOVE

*T*his is a good after-supper family activity in summer while it's still light. One person (parent or older child) starts out with chalk to make a trail of small arrows on the sidewalk. He can go around the block or any other safe route, ending at a store, a friend's house, or even back home. After ten minutes, the other family members follow the arrow trail until they catch up with the one they love.

♥ 354 BABY TALK

*T*ell a child about her infancy and the time before her birth. Share your feelings about how much she was wanted. Show her the baby book and the cards and lists of gifts that came from those who also loved her. Remind her of how cute and cuddly she was—*and is*!

♥ 355 NAP TIME-OUT

*N*o matter what the age of your child, a short nap can help you both cool down when you feel that anger is setting in. Set a timer for ten to fifteen minutes and, together, quickly stretch out on a couch or bed. This kind of time-out often brings about a calm, loving solution to the problem.

♥ 356 LOVE CASSETTE

*M*ake a tape to send to a faraway friend or relative, or to one of the kids' friends who's moved away. Tell the latest news, jokes, successes and failures, what the pets are doing, movies seen, and so forth. Making the tape just like a friendly chat will help kids overcome self-consciousness. Show how to use the pause control to stop the tape while you think of the next thing you want to say. Remember to send a love message at the end.

♥ 357 FANTASTIC STORIES

*C*reate stories for young children using repetition. Try beginning a made-up story with the same first line each night. For example, begin the story "One day when you were flying along in your space ship . . . ." Then make the following lines different each night. Create some fantasy characters, too. One might be Michelle (your child's name), who is President of the United States or owner of a dinosaur farm. Read *Baby's Bedtime Book* (Kay Choroa, Dutton, 1984).

♥ 358 TIGHT HUGS

With a child in your lap, practice tight hugs, the kind that get arms all tangled together and bodies close as glue on paper. Sometimes it's fun to see if another person can pull you apart. Remind a child that when he is afraid, he should think of your tight hug enfolding him.

♥ 359 SUGGESTION TIME

On a regular basis, ask kids for their suggestions for the family. Even young children will have some good ideas. Asking children for an opinion shows that you respect and love them. Here are some ideas for suggestions a parent can elicit: how to save money, how to spend money, bed times, excursions, menus, gifts, room arrangement, clothing purchases, places to keep the house key. Don't tell a child that her suggestion is impractical, just be grateful for the input. Thank the suggestor and try to use as many as reasonably possible.

♥ 360 A TRUE LOVE STORY

*B*ecky and Jeff knew that this Christmas was going to be different because Dad had been laid off and Mom's job paid little. In talking it over as a family, the kids reluctantly decided that the gifts they most needed were clothes, since they were both growing so fast. While Jeff didn't think much of the clothes idea, he didn't like his ankles showing because his pants were too short. So he grumblingly agreed that they'd all go together to the after-Christmas sales and find good buys.

When Jeff said, "You mean there won't be any gifts under the tree?" his mom answered, "Perhaps some small things from the relatives, but we'll have a good Christmas just the same—just wait and see. We can go caroling in the neighborhood, skiing in the woods at the edge of town, make decorations, be in the pageant at church, and have a potluck Christmas Eve dinner with aunties, uncles, and cousins."

But Becky was concerned about Jeff, who had just turned nine. "After all," she thought, "he's still a kid and should get the toy he really wants." It was a new train engine to replace the one that had burned out last Christmas, and Becky hoped that the small amount of money she'd squirreled away from babysitting might be enough to buy the engine.

Jeff didn't have any savings, but he did want to give something to Becky; having a teen-age sister wasn't as bad as his friends said it would be. When they'd been at the mall, she had looked longingly at some ski poles and he thought maybe he could buy them if he shoveled enough sidewalks.

Happily, it snowed regularly in the days before Christmas, and by saving all his earnings, he was only ten dollars away from his goal. At the same time, Becky was frequently babysitting for the neighbors, but her train-engine fund, too, was still a little short.

* * *

Christmas Eve seemed almost like the old days—the big turkey Mom had been given as a gift from her employer was stuffed, cooked to a golden brown, and regally set at the end of the table. Relatives arrived with vegetables and salads and Christmas desserts. There were games and carols, and the cousins went outside for a snowball fight. When the party was over, Becky and Jeff noticed a few small gifts and one really big box left under the tree, so they went to bed anticipating Christmas morning. Just before bed, Jeff hid the ski poles in the front hall closet, and when Becky was sure everyone was asleep, she put the wrapped engine under the tree.

Early Christmas morning, Becky and Jeff heard their parents preparing the traditional breakfast of Christmas coffee cake, juice, and decorated cookies. The parents kissed their children and presented them with hand-made red and green certificates for their new clothes. Then the little gifts from the relatives were opened—perfume and stationery and belts and a game—really thoughtful choices for all of them.

Only the mysterious big box and the engine were left to be opened. But Jeff insisted on presenting his gift first—and he couldn't imagine why Becky burst into tears when she saw the ski poles. She wiped her eyes and shoved the engine box toward him, and she was surprised to see him frown and bite his lip when he unwrapped the new engine. Their parents looked at them for some explanation, so Becky admitted she'd sold her skis at the ski shop in order to have enough money for the engine. Then Jeff said that he'd sold his train track to his friend Billy Shuster so he could buy the poles! They were all laughing and crying together when Dad suggested that they open the big box. Aunt Louise had put a note on it: "This isn't new, but I know you don't have one, and I think you can use it." What could it be?

They all sat silently looking at a sewing machine. Then suddenly the ideas flowed. Mom said it would be a lot less expensive to buy patterns and fabric than to buy readymade clothes—so there could be money left over. Dad said he had learned sewing in high school and would teach the kids how to use the machine. With the money left over, they could buy back the train tracks and get secondhand skis.

That's just what they did! Dad showed Jeff how to make cuffs for his jeans, Becky made him some great shirts, Mom helped Becky make some trendy clothes. Since the owner of the ski shop hadn't sold the skis yet, Becky got them back and went skiing with her friends. It turned out that Billy Shuster received a new train set for Christmas, so he sold Jeff's tracks back to him.

And, best yet, there was much laughter and love in the house as the family celebrated a most curious Christmas.

♥ 361 GOOD-NIGHT EVERY NIGHT

*T*ry not to miss wishing your child "good sleep," "sweet dreams," "happy waking up." You may have to telephone it if you're on a business trip, or interrupt your favorite TV program, or excuse yourself for a few moments when you have company. Remember that this won't always be possible when kids leave home, so do it while you can.

♥ 362 "TRIPLE T" TUCKING IN

*R*eally tuck in a child. Bring the covers up around his shoulders and make them snug around his body, down to his toes. This kind of hands-on cuddling is similar to snuggling or swaddling a baby. Kids love it, especially if you make it fun. Youngsters look forward to "Triple T" (Tuck-Tuck-Time), then a kiss and to sleep.

♥ 363 NO MATTER WHAT

*L*ove is not withheld because a youngster has been disobedient or lazy or has disappointed you in some way. If the day has put a strain on parent-child relationships so that you haven't had the time to verbally express your love, bedtime is the perfect opportunity. Try love messages such as these: "You are so special to me." "No one could ever take your place." "You make me happy in so many ways." "I may not always *like* some things you do, but I'll always *love* you." "I love you no matter what!"

♥ 364 DAY'S END

A wise minister once told a newlywed couple, "Never let the day end in anger." While you may not immediately solve the problem that brought on the anger toward your spouse, you should always reaffirm your love at day's end—and you'll be surprised that the problem often solves itself. The same is true about an angry exchange with a child. At day's end, be sure to express your love.

♥ 365 WHATSOEVER THINGS

T oo often a family gives all its attention to problems, forgetting the good things that happen during the day. Before an older child goes to bed, or in tucking in a young child, talk about something good or loving that happened. Take your clue from the Bible, Paul's words in Philippians, chapter 4, verse 8: "Whatsoever things are true, whatsoever things are honest, whatsoever things are just, whatsoever things are pure, whatsoever things are lovely, whatsoever things are of good report; if there be any virtue, and if there be any praise, think on these things" (King James Version). Thinking on these "whatsoever things" will put a smile on the face of both parent and child.

INDEX

The number following the entry is the number of the idea, not the page number.